Fabulous Western Canada

Capture the excitement of the **Great West**!

D0004556

Ulysses Travel Guides

Research and Writing (Extracts From Ulysses Guide *Western Canada*)
Tracey Arial, Julie Brodeur, Pierre Daveluy, Alexis de Gheldère, Daniel Desjardins, Paul-Éric Dumontier, Jacqueline Grekin, Mark Heard, Stéphanie Heindenreich, Paul Karr, Rodolphe Lasnes, Pierre Longnus, Jennifer McMorran, Lorette Pierson, Corinne Pohlmann, François Rémillard, Marylène Têtu

Associate Editor
Pierre Ledoux

Copy Editing and Translation
Matthew McLauchlin

Artistic Director
Pascal Biet

Iconographic Research
Julie Brodeur, Annie Gilbert, Christian Lambert, Amber Martin

Cartographers
Kirill Berdnikov, Philippe Thomas

Computer Graphics
Marie-France Denis, Isabelle Lalonde

Photography
Cover Page
Moraine Lake, Banff National Park, Alberta
© John E Marriott / Alamy

This work was produced under the direction of Olivier Gougeon.

Acknowledgements
Ulysses Travel Guides would like to give special thanks to Pierre Longnus; Philippe Renault; Don Boynton and Laureen Dirksen, Travel Alberta; Judy Miller, Tourism Saskatchewan; Stephanie Bachewich, Travel Manitoba; Lynn Lafontaine, Library and Archives Canada.

Allen Sawchuck, Inglis Grain Elevators National Historic Site; Jen Wintoniw, Mennonite Heritage Village; Shelley Myhres, St. Ann's Academy National Historic Site; Karen Cook, Kootenay Rockies Tourism; Danielle Currie, Vancouver Art Gallery; Kiersten Drysdale, Folk Arts Council of Winnipeg; Laurie Reed, Friends of Fort Steele Society at Fort Steele Heritage Town; Britt Burnham, Royal BC Museum; Jennifer Webb, UBC Museum of Anthropology; Graham Bell, The Butchart Gardens Ltd.; Timothy L. Lynch, Tourism Kelowna; Carolyn Bonnick, District of Hudson's Hope; Andrew Loveridge, Galiano Island Infocentre; Vanessa Murphy, Tourism Whistler; Kerry Stansfield, Penticton & Wine Country Tourism; Karen, Telegraph Cove Resort; Karen Cameron, Northern BC Film Commission; Gladys Atrill, Town of Smithers; Kim Barrows, Tourism Powell River; April Cheng, North Cariboo Tourism, Quesnel Community & Economic Development Corporation; Andrew Webber, Regional District of Kitimat-Stikine; Lana Kingston, Tourism Vancouver Island; Randle Robertson, The Burgess Shale Geoscience Foundation; Peter Reath, viewcalgary.com; Kevin Nienhuis, Edmonton Tourism / Edmonton Economic Development Corporation; Nicky Peeters, Fort Calgary; Lena Goon, Whyte Museum of the Canadian Rockies; Cynthia Blackmore, Reynolds-Alberta Museum; Kimberly Evans, West Edmonton Mall; Andrea Busse, Saskatchewan Environment; Marie-Josée Leblanc, Blue Metropolis Foundation; Jenny Jasper, VIA Rail Canada; Antony Thériault, Parks Canada; Craig Larsen, Softwood Exportation Council; Antony Pacey, Canada Science and Technology Museum Corporation; Susan Kooyman, Glenbow Archives; Angela McManus, Cedar Creek Estate Winery; William Manzer, Canada Post Corporation; Brenda Jones, Vancouver Aquarium; Robin Sharpe, Barkerville Historic Town; Pat Reece, yukoninfo.com; Lisa Cameron, British Columbia Wine Institute; Jennifer Rhyne, Vancouver, Coast & Mountains Tourism Region; François Ricard, Fonds Gabrielle Roy; Matthew G. Wheeler; Jack Rowand; Lonnie Wishart; Tom Ryan.

We acknowledge the financial support of the Government of Canada through the Book Publishing Industry Development Program (BPIDP) for our publishing activities. We would also like to thank the Government of Québec – Tax credit for book publishing – Administered by SODEC.

Bibliothèque et Archives nationales du Québec and Library and Archives Canada cataloguing in publication

Main entry under title :
    Fabulous Western Canada
    (Fabulous)
    Translation of: Fabuleux Ouest canadien.
    Includes index.
    ISBN 978-2-89464-875-9
    1. Canada, Western - Guidebooks. I. Series.

FC3233.F3213 2008   917.1204'4   C2008-940524-2

▶ Alberta's countryside.
© iStockphoto.com / Jason Verschoor

▲ A rural landscape with the Rockies in the background. © iStockphoto.com / Andrew Penner

Attraction Classification

★   Interesting
★ ★   Worth a visit
★ ★ ★   Not to be missed

List of Maps

Map Symbols

✈	International airport	▲	Mountain
✛	Regional airport	🌳	Park
♀	Church	◐	Beach
H	Hospital	☀	Lookout
🚆	Train station	🏌	Golf course
🚌	Bus station	🚗	Car ferry
◣	Glacier	🚢	Passenger ferry
ⓘ	Tourist information		

▶ The glass and steel towers of Calgary.
© iStockphoto.com / Jeff Whyte

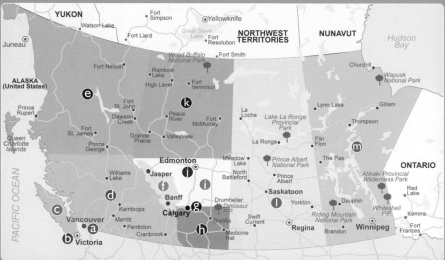

Regions Covered by this Guide

a. Vancouver

b. Victoria and Surroundings

c. Vancouver Island and the Southern Gulf Islands

d. Southern British Columbia

e. Northern British Columbia

f. The Rocky Mountains

g. Calgary

h. Southern Alberta

i. Central Alberta

j. Edmonton

k. Northern Alberta

l. Saskatchewan

m. Manitoba

Portrait

GEOGRAPHY

Western Canada is a difficult region to pin down. Some define it as British Columbia and Alberta, some as everything west of Ontario (generally thought of as central Canada), while still others would further divide that version of Western Canada into the Prairies, the mountains and the coast. This guidebook uses the wider definition, including the provinces of British Columbia, Alberta, Saskatchewan and Manitoba, so that we may introduce you to the range of landscapes found across this part of Canada. The majestic chain of mountains, the Rockies, is an easy focus for any trip to this part of the world. But what trip to Canada's West would be complete without also experiencing Calgary and the world-famous Stampede, the rolling plains, magnificent lakes and rivers of southern Alberta, Saskatchewan and Manitoba, the Pacific metropolis of Vancouver, the stunning coastline, the Gulf Islands or the fruitful valleys of southern British Columbia?

This region has only been known to Europeans for 200 years. In fact, the sons of the French explorer La Vérendrye did not set eyes on the Rocky Mountains until the end of the 18th century, and England's George Vancouver only explored the Pacific coast and Columbia River in the last decade of the same century. White settlement of the region is even more recent, going back just over 100 years in Alberta, which, like Saskatchewan, has only existed as a province since 1905. Aboriginal peoples have inhabited this territory for at least 11,000 years, but never in large numbers; there were only 220,000 of them in all of Canada when explorer Jacques Cartier arrived in Québec in 1534.

As we said, this guide covers the four most westerly provinces of Canada: British Columbia, located on the Pacific coast and covered by vast mountain chains; Alberta, which begins on the eastern slopes of the Rocky Mountains and extends into the vast Canadian prairies; Saskatchewan; and finally Manitoba, which borders the central province of Ontario. From the coast eastward, these provinces are bordered to the south by the U.S. states of Washington, Idaho, Montana, North Dakota and Minnesota. British Columbia borders Alaska to the northwest and the Yukon to the north. The northeastern corner of British Columbia and the entire northern border of Alberta and Saskatchewan are shared with the Northwest Territories, while Manitoba's northern border is shared by the Inuit territory of Nunavut.

British Columbia is the largest of these provinces with an area of 950,000km^2. Alberta covers 660,000km^2, Saskatchewan stretches over 651,900km^2, and Manitoba, the smallest of Canada's western provinces, covers some 650,000km^2.

Carved out by countless fjords and dotted with hundreds of islands, British Columbia's jagged coastline is 7,000km long, not counting the shores of the islands. The largest of these is Vancouver Island, about the size of the Netherlands and home to the provincial capital, Victoria. Despite its name, the city of Vancouver is not on the island

▲ The Canadian West during the British colonial period. © *Archives Canada, NMC-141864*

but rather lies across the Strait of Juan de Fuca, on the mainland. The Queen Charlotte Islands or Haida Gwaii lie to the north. The maritime nature of the province is foremost in many minds, but in actuality three quarters of the province lies an average of more than 930m above sea level, and a 3,000m-high barrier of mountains is visible from the coast. From west to east, a succession of mountain ranges stretches all the way to the famous Rocky Mountains, whose summits reach up to 4,000m. This chain was named for its bare, rocky eastern slopes.

During the Precambrian era, the Pacific Ocean covered most of Western Canada. Over a period of about 500 million years, the ocean advanced and receded, depositing sediment on the Precambrian rock of the Canadian Shield, one of the oldest rock formations on earth. Microscopic organisms in the sea died, creating enormous amounts of decaying organic matter, at the source of Alberta's huge oil deposits. By the Cretaceous period, some 75 million years ago, the Arctic Ocean had flooded most of Alberta, creating a vast inland sea known as the Bearpaw.

▲ A dinosaur skeleton. © *Travel Alberta*

Dinosaurs thrived along the shores of this subtropical sea and along the rivers that emptied into it. They lived there for millions of years until about 70 million years ago, when the Pacific Plate collided with the North American Plate and was forced upwards, forming the mountain ranges of present-day British Columbia and western Alberta. This gradually altered the climate, cooling things down and eventually killing off the dinosaurs around 63 million years ago. Then, about a million years ago, four polar ice caps advanced across the region, eroding the mountain ranges and carving out the rivers and lakes that make up the present landscape of Alberta, Sakatchewan and Manitoba as they receded.

These rivers divide the province of Alberta into distinct regions. The Mackenzie, Peace and Athabasca Rivers make the land arable as far as the Boreal forests of the north and eventually empty into the Arctic Ocean. The North Saskatchewan and Red Deer Rivers provide most of the irrigation for Alberta farms, and empty into Hudson Bay, along with the South Saskatchewan, Oldman and Bow Rivers.

THE FIRST INHABITANTS

The region's first human inhabitants are believed to have arrived at least 11,000 years ago when the Wisconsin glacier receded, though they may have arrived on the American continent earlier. These people found large numbers of buffalo and other game animals here, as well as berries and roots. They did not waste any of these resources, using hides for clothing, storage and shelter, bones as tools, horns for spoons, antlers for handles, plants for medicines, sinew for thread and clay for pottery.

There is some doubt, however, as to whether native civilization on the West Coast came with these same vast waves of immigration. According to one theory, the ancestors of the West Coast tribes came here more recently (around 3000 BC) from islands in the Pacific. Proponents of this hypothesis base their argument on Aboriginal art, traditions and languages, which are not unlike those of the indigenous peoples of the Pacific islands.

In the 18th century, five First Nations occupied the area between Hudson Bay and the Rocky Mountains. The part of the Canadian Shield covered by vast forests is Ojibway land. The Assiniboine occupied the plains and prairies, while the Western Cree lived in the forests and plains south of present-day Manitoba and Saskatchewan. Southwest of these two groups lived the Blackfoot, and in the far north, the Athapaskans. The arrival of the European colonization dras-

▲ Treaty negotiations between Europeans and Aboriginal people. © *Glenbow Archives; NA-40-1*

ALBERTA TREATIES

Under Treaty No. 6, the Cree, Assiniboine and Ojibwa surrendered all lands in central Alberta in 1876. The next year, the Blackfoot, Blood, Peigan, Sarcee and Stoney signed Treaty No. 7, surrendering all lands south of Treaty No. 6. The northern lands of the Beaver, Cree, Slavey and Chipewyan were surrendered in Treaty No. 8, signed in 1899.

tically disrupted these nations. They were either brought into direct conflict with the colonists or other displaced Aboriginal groups, or were affected by the ensuing profound changes in the environment, such as the near extinction of the Prairie buffalo herds.

THE ARRIVAL OF THE EUROPEANS

Canadian history is marked by a series of treaties between First Nations and Europeans. In the West, the first treaties were drawn up in the 19th century, when the Aboriginal peoples, seeing themselves on the brink of assimilation, had to give up much of their land to the Crown. This is when the first reserves were created, which, to this day, are still home to many First Nation's peoples. In most cases, the area set aside for reserves was based on five inhabitants per square mile (around 2.5km²).

When the first Europeans arrived on the coast in the 18th century, the territory that was to become British Columbia

was occupied by Nootka, Coast Salish, Kwakiutl, Bella Coola, Tsimshian, Haida and Tlingit. Tagish, Tahltan, Testsaut, Carrier, Chilcotin, Interior Salish, Nicola and Kootenay occupied the interior. Slavery seems to have been practised among the Interior Salish, who had three social classes.

The region that would become Vancouver was inhabited by the Salish (the other linguistic families on the Pacific coast are the Haida, the Tsimshian, the Tlingit, the Nootka, the Kwakiutl and the Bella Coola). Like their compatriots, they favoured this region for its remarkably mild climate and abundance of belugas, salmon, seals, fruit and other resources. This beneficial environment, combined with the barrier formed by the nearby mountains, enabled the coastal nations to thrive. Not only was their population quite large, but it was also significantly denser than that of other First Nations in central and eastern Canada.

In 1820, there were some 25,000 Salish living on the shores of the Fraser River, from its mouth south of Vancouver all the way up into the Rockies. Like other native tribes, the Salish were sedentary and lived in villages of red cedar longhouses. They traded with other natives along the coast during potlatches, festive ceremonies lasting weeks on end and marked by the exchange of gifts.

FUR AND EXPLORATION

In 1670, the region now known as the prairies, made up of the provinces of Manitoba, Saskatchewan and Alberta, was ceded by the British Crown to the

▼ Aboriginal people of the Salish nation. © *Glenbow Archives; NA-2069-5*

THE HUDSON'S BAY COMPANY

In 1610, English navigator Henry Hudson discovered the strait and the bay that would bear his name. Hudson Bay opens on to the Labrador Sea and the Atlantic Ocean through the Hudson Strait, north of what is now Québec.

During the late 1650s, Médard Chouart Des Groseillers and his brother-in-law Pierre-Esprit Radisson, brave fur traders, or *coureurs des bois*, organized an expedition that took them west of Lake Superior. They failed however to reach Hudson Bay, which the Cree had described to them in detail. In 1665 in London, contrary to all expectations, they met King Charles II and shared with him the secret of Hudson Bay's riches. He decided to equip them with two ships. Radisson's ran aground, but the *Nonsuch*, under the command of Des Groseillers, managed to enter the Hudson Strait and Hudson Bay in 1668.

In 1670, what would later become the Hudson's Bay Company was founded under the name "The Governor and Company of Adventurers of England, trading into Hudson's Bay," with the permission of the king. Within a few years, it controlled most of northern Québec and Ontario, all of Manitoba, virtually all of Saskatchewan, the southern half of Alberta and a large portion of the Northwest Territories: this huge territory was known as Rupert's Land. Following an 1857 parliamentary investigation, the company was forced to hand over the southern portion of what are now Alberta, Saskatchewan and Manitoba to Canada. In 1869, it relinquished ownership of Rupert's Land.

In 1912, the Hudson's Bay Company planned to open a chain of department stores in Western Canada. By the 1970s, it had a store in every major Canadian city and suburb. From a simple fur trading company, over the years the Hudson's Bay Company, Canada's oldest company, became a major multinational enterprise and one of the most successful retailers in the country: The Bay.

▲   An old Hudson's Bay Company trading post.
    © *Glenbow Archives; NA-2750-1*

ALEXANDER MACKENZIE

Alexander Mackenzie was born in Scotland in 1764. He immigrated to New York in 1774 with his father, who joined the British Army while the American War of Independence was being waged. After the death of his mother in 1778, he was sent to Montréal, a major fur trade hub. Influenced by what he saw, he left school in 1779 to become a fur trader himself.

▲ Alexander Mackenzie.
© Glenbow Archives; NA-1733-1

He cut his teeth in the trade, and then in 1784 the company he was working for sent him to Detroit as a merchant. Mackenzie showed leadership and business acumen, and the company offered him a partnership to move into Aboriginal territory—Northwestern Canada—in the spring of 1785.

Mackenzie's company merged with the North West Company, and in 1788 he was sent to the Athabasca region, in the northern part of what is now Alberta.

In 1789, Mackenzie's first expedition left from Fort Chipewyan on the Athabasca River. Eight hundred and fifty kilometres into his descent of the Athabasca River, Mackenzie realized that it led to a larger river flowing toward the Arctic Ocean, and not the Pacific, after a perilous 1,650-km journey. This major river, which he spent two weeks following until its end, is now called the Mackenzie River in his honour.

In 1792, Mackenzie set out on a second expedition. Heeding the advice of Aboriginal acquaintances, this time he tried his luck on the Peace River. Mackenzie and his fellow travellers crossed lakes and rivers, facing treacherous rapids and difficult portages and stopping often to patch their heavily laden canoe. He then had to cross part of the territory by land, ending up at the Bella Coola River, by which they reached the Pacific Ocean in July 1793.

In 1802, Mackenzie became Sir Alexander Mackenzie. A short while later, he returned to Scotland, where he married and fathered three children. Sir Alexander Mackenzie died in 1820.

Hudson's Bay Company, which took over the economic and political administration of the region.

The Hudson's Bay Company controlled trade in Rupert's Land, which encompassed all land that drained into Hudson Bay, much of present-day Canada. Hudson's Bay Company traders, however, accused French fur trappers or *voyageurs* of unfair competition because they headed inland to the source of the fur instead of waiting for the natives to bring the pelts to the trading posts.

In 1691, Hudson's Bay Company employee Henry Kelsey was the first to set sight on the eastern boundary of Alberta. Encouraged by favourable reports, independent fur traders in Montréal formed the North West Company in 1787, and then founded the first trading post in Alberta, Fort Chipewyan on Lake Athabasca.

These trading posts eventually came to serve as bases for exploration, and in 1792 Alexander Mackenzie crossed Alberta by the Peace River, becoming the first European to reach the Pacific overland through North America. The trading companies' sole interest in the West lay in the fur trade, which continued unabated, even receiving a boost when the North West and Hudson's Bay companies merged in 1821. By the late 1860s, however, beaver stocks had begun to dwindle, and merchants turned their attention to buffalo. After only 10 years of buffalo hunting and trading, there were almost no more of these majestic animals which had once roamed wild.

THE MARCH WEST

The fur-trading companies were only interested in fur and offered nothing in the way of law enforcement. Whisky traders from the United States were thus drawn north to this lawless land. With dwindling buffalo herds, Aboriginal peoples were exploited and generally taken advantage of by the Americans, not to mention the deleterious effect the whisky trade had on them. Various uprisings, including the Cypress Hills Massacre, prompted the formation of the North West Mounted Police and set the stage for the March West. Heading out from Fort Garry in Winnipeg, the police crossed the plains, led by James Macleod. Their presence got rid of the whisky traders at Fort Whoop-Up in

▼ North West Mounted Police detachment at Fort Macleod. © *Archives Canada; NMC-141864*

1874, and they then set about establishing four forts in southern Alberta, including Fort Macleod and Fort Calgary.

AMERICAN IMPULSES

The fur trade being the principal activity of the Hudson's Bay Company, the Company did all it could to discourage colonization in the region, so that they could pursue their activities unimpeded. At the time, the United States had just ended its civil war and was clearly interested in conquering British North America, present-day Canada. They had purchased Alaska from Russia in 1867, and in 1868, Minnesota drew up a resolution favouring the annexation of the Canadian prairies.

These vague American impulses were enough to worry the leaders of the fledgling Canadian Confederation (1867), who negotiated with Great Britain and the Hudson's Bay Company to acquire the Northwest Territories in 1868.

THE METIS

The annexation of the Northwest Territories was done without so much as consulting the people who had settled there, for the most part French-speaking Metis. These people resisted and prevented the governor appointed by Canada from taking power.

Their leader, Louis Riel, tried to obtain a land title for his people, but the Canadian government paid no attention. With his troops, Riel then declared himself leader of Manitoba and forced

Ottawa to negotiate. Finally, on July 15, 1870, the bilingual province of Manitoba was created. Its territory was small not much larger than present-day Belgium, and except for some control over land development and natural resources, it had little of the power the other provinces had. These circumstances have continued to influence relations between the federal government and what are now the Prairie provinces of Manitoba, Saskatchewan and Alberta.

Some 15 years later, the Metis called back their exiled leader to confront a similar situation, this time in Saskatchewan. Ottawa was faring better this time and sent troops to quash the rebellion. Under of an old British law, Riel was found guilty of treason and hanged in 1885.

▶ Louis Riel. © Glenbow Archives; NA-2631-2

▲   An extended Metis family in their community. © *Archives Canada; PA-044328*

THE ISOLATION OF THE PACIFIC COAST

In 1792, George Vancouver (1757-1798) took possession of the territory surrounding the city that now bears his name for the King of Great Britain, thereby putting an end to any claims the Russians and Spaniards planned to make. The former would have liked to extend their empire southward from Alaska, while the latter, firmly entrenched in California, were looking northward. Spanish explorers had even made a brief trip into Burrard Inlet in the 16th century. This far-flung region was not coveted enough to cause any bloody wars, however, and was left undeveloped for years to come.

The Vancouver region was hard to reach not only by sea, but also by land, with the virtually insurmountable obstacle of the Rocky Mountains blocking the way. Imagine setting out across the immense North American continent from Montréal, following the lakes and rivers of the Canadian Shield, and exhausting yourself crossing the endless Prairies, only to end up barred from the Pacific by a wall of rock several thousand metres high. In 1808, the fabulously wealthy fur merchant and adventurer Simon Fraser became the first person to reach the site of Vancouver from inland. This belated breakthrough had little impact on the region, though, since Fraser was unable to reach any trade agreements with the coastal nations and quickly withdrew to his trading posts in the Rockies.

The Salish thus continued to lead a peaceful existence here for many more years before being intruded upon by white settlers. In 1808, except for spor-

THE RUSSIAN PRESENCE

When Alexander Mackenzie reached the Pacific in 1793, other Europeans had made it there before him. England's Captain Portlock had reached Nootka Sound in 1786, eight years after Captain Cook had moored his ship there, only to find that the Russians had already settled there. In fact, Russians from the coasts of Siberia had created a vast island empire that included the Aleutians, Sitka Island, and Kodiak Island. Their ships had been sailing between Siberia and Alaska for some time to trade with Aboriginal peoples, who sold them beaver pelts, which were very popular at the time.

Even Spain was familiar with this part of the Northwest. In 1774, Spanish explorer Juan Pérez sailed north from Monterey, California, with orders to take possession of the territories of the northern coast of North America in the name of the Spanish Crown and to report back on the presence of the Russians in that territory.

At the end of the 18th century, the British and the Spanish in the area were at the brick of war. The British had entered an area where the Spanish expected to find only the Russians. In 1789, after Captain Martínez unwigely seized Captain Colnett's ships, the British threatened the Spanish with reprisals if they did not give them equal access to trade on the northwest coast. As a result, the Russians, the Spanish and the British shared the region, with the Spanish later retreating to the south. Thus, British and Russian flags flew over the northwestern coast in 1793.

In 1825, Russia and the United Kingdom signed a treaty: the border was established at the 141st meridian, up to the north at the 60th parallel. But in 1867, the United States bought the territory of Alaska from Russia, requiring the Hudson's Bay Company to leave the border region. The territorial dispute pitting the United States against Canada (then a British dominion) and more specifically British Columbia, would be resolved only in 1907.

adic visits by Russians, Spaniards and Britons looking to trade pelts for fabrics and objects from the Orient, the Aboriginal people were still living according to the traditions handed down to them by their ancestors. In fact, European influence on their lifestyle remained negligible until the mid-19th century, at which point colonization of the territory began slowly.

In 1818, Great Britain and the United States created the condominium of Oregon, a vast fur-trading zone along the Pacific bounded by California to the south and Alaska to the north. In so doing, these two countries excluded the Russians and the Spanish from this region once and for all. The employees of the North West Company combed the valley of the Fraser River in search of furs. Not only did they encounter the coastal Aboriginals, whose precious resources they were depleting, but they also had to adapt to the tumultuous waterways of the Rockies, which made travelling by canoe nearly impossible. In 1827, after the Hudson's Bay Company took over the North West Company, a large fur-trading post was founded at Fort Langley, on the shores of the Fraser, some 90km east of the present site of Vancouver, which would remain untouched for several more decades.

▼ A fur merchant with his cargo. © *Archives Canada; C-001229*

CANADIAN CONFEDERATION

Unlike the Prairies, which were simply annexed to the Canadian Confederation in 1868, British Columbia was already a British colony and was thus able to negotiate its entrance into Confederation. Isolated on the Pacific coast, British Columbia's principal trading partner was California. As its population grew with the 1858 gold rush, certain residents even dreamed of creating an independent country. But these hopes were dashed at the end of this prosperous period, when in 1871, British Columbia's population was only 36,000. Great Britain had already joined its colony on Vancouver Island with the colony of New Caledonia on the British Columbia mainland in anticipation of their eventual integration into the new Canadian Confederation.

With a promise from Canada that a pan-Canadian railway would reach the coast by 1881, British Columbia joined Confederation in 1871. However, all sorts of problems delayed the construction of the railroad, and in 1873, as a severe recession gripped Canada and caused major delays in the railway,

British Columbia threatened to separate. It wasn't until November 7, 1885 that the railway from Montréal to Port Moody (20km from Vancouver) was finally completed, four years late.

EXPANDING CONFEDERATION

As the railway expanded, more and more farmers settled in the region known as the Northwest Territories, which had no responsible government on the provincial level. You will recall that Canada had annexed the territories (Prairies) without giving them provincial status, except for a small parcel of land that became the province of Manitoba. Inevitably, Canada had to create the provinces of Alberta and Saskatchewan and enlarge the province of Manitoba in 1905.

Most settlers arrived in Alberta when the Canadian Pacific Railway reached Fort Calgary in 1883 and eight years later in 1891 when the Grand Trunk Railway's northern route reached Edmonton. Ranchers from the United States and Canada initially grabbed up huge tracts of land with grazing leases; in the case of the Cochrane Ranch, west of Calgary, the lease occupied 40,000ha. Much of this open range land was eventually granted to homesteaders.

To easterners, the West was ranches, rodeos and cheap land, but the reality was more often a sod hut and loneliness. Though a homestead could be registered for $10, a homesteader first had to cultivate the land, and own a certain number of head of cattle. But the endless potential for a better future

▼ A Western homesteader's cabin.
© *Glenbow Archives; NA-2061-10*

THE TRANSCONTINENTAL RAILROAD

▲ An old CPR steam locomotive.
© Archives Canada; PA-143158

On July 1, 1867, Canadian Confederation brought together three colonies in eastern British North America to form a new country. Nova Scotia and New Brunswick were to be linked via railroad to Quebec and Ontario. Then in 1870, Manitoba was formed. British Columbia, on the West Coast, would join Confederation in 1871, with the promise that a transcontinental railroad would be built within 10 years to connect it to eastern Canada.

In 1880, with the 10-year deadline rapidly approaching, a decision was made to use the American method in the Rockies: lay as much track as fast as possible and hire Chinese immigrants to do the work. Construction along the steep, slippery gorges was particularly difficult, and many hundreds of workers lost their lives.

The Canadian Pacific Railway Company (CPR) was formed on February 16, 1881, with George Stephen as its first president. General manager William Cornelius Van Horne supervised work across the Prairies and the Rockies. He eventually asked Thomas G. Shaughnessy to join him in managing the company to complete the work.

One of the heads of the CPR after 1883, Donald A. Smith, ceremonially drove the last spike at Craigellachie, British Columbia on November 7, 1885. The first train left Dalhousie Station in Montréal on June 28, 1886. With its 150 passengers, it arrived at Port Moody Station (20km from Vancouver: the first train would reach the city's new station the following year) on July 4, 1886, after travelling 4,655km in 139 hours. Shortly thereafter, the West Coast was linked to the East Coast: with Shaughnessy's help, in 1889 Van Horne succeeded in building the railroad from coast to coast, through the American state of Maine to Saint John, New Brunswick.

▲ A Grand Trunk Railway train leaving Calgary. © *Canada Science and Technology Museum; CN002394*

kept people coming from far and wide. Alberta's population rose from 73,000 in 1901 to 375,000 in 1911.

HARD TIMES

Life in Western Canada was hard around the turn of the 20th century. The coal mines of Alberta and British Columbia were the most dangerous in the Americas: by the end of the 19th century there were 23 fatal accidents for every million tonnes of coal extracted, while in the United States there were only six. For the farmers who came here to grow wheat, the high cost of rail transport, lack of rail service, low wheat prices and bad harvests, along with duties too high to protect the fledgling industry in central Canada, all came together to make for miserable and desperate times.

In British Columbia, a strike by 7,000 miners looking to improve their working conditions lasted two years, from 1912 to 1914, and was finally broken by the Canadian army. Certain arrangements improved the situation, and the First World War created a temporary boom which lasted until 1920, causing a rise in the price of raw materials and wheat.

The workers remained dissatisfied, though, and in 1919, the workers' unions of the West created their own central union, the One Big Union. As supporters of Russian Bolsheviks, the union's goal was to abolish capitalism. However, a general strike in Winnipeg, Manitoba quickly created a rift between the workers with respect to their objectives, and demonstrated Canada's determination not to let the country adopt Marxist ideology. The 1920s again proved prosperous for the West, and Alberta and the prairie provinces, whose economies were essentially agricultural at the time, were able to finish clearing their territory.

The great crash of 1929 had a profound effect on Western Canada, in particular the Prairie provinces, which saw their agricultural revenues drop by 94% between 1929 and 1933! And the fact that their farms specialized almost exclusively in wheat made the situation even worse.

SOCIAL CREDIT AND THE CCF

This period was marked by the evolution of two Western Canadian political movements, both of which remained almost exclusively local, Social Credit and the Co-operative Commonwealth Federation (CCF). The doctrine of the Social Credit, which supported the small farmers' and workers' stand against the capitalist ascendancy by providing interest-free credit, reached its height under William Aberhart, who was elected premier of Alberta in 1935. His government dared to defy the capitalist system like no Canadian government ever had before (or has since). In 1936, Alberta refused to redeem any bonds, unilaterally cut the interest it was paying on its loans in half, started printing its own money, prohibited the seizure of assets for non-payment and even went so far as to force provincial newspapers to print the government's point of view.

One by one, these Albertan laws were voided by the federal government or the Supreme Court of Canada, but Aberhart was so successful in making the population believe it was the victim of a conspiracy involving the federal government and capitalists that he was re-elected in 1940. He died in 1943 and was replaced by Ernest Manning, elected in 1944. Manning got the party in order and eliminated all the anti-capitalist rhetoric from the party line. He dealt with all the controversy surrounding Alberta's debt, enabling the province to benefit once again from investment capital. In 1947, large oil deposits were discovered, and from then on the province enjoyed unprecedented prosperity, thanks to royalties and foreign investment in the gas and petroleum industries.

For its part, the CCF reached its pinnacle in British Columbia in 1933 when it became the official opposition. An outgrowth of the Socialist Party, workers' unions and farmers' associations, the party was brought to power in Saskatchewan in 1944 with the election of North America's first socialist government under Premier Tommy Douglas, who introduced a public healthcare insurance plan during his term of office. The CCF eventually gave rise to the New Democratic Party (NDP).

▼   William Aberhart. © *Glenbow Archives; NB-16-217*

▲   Ernest Manning. © *Glenbow Archives; ND-3-7109b*

THE OIL BOOM

Neither the Social Credit nor the CCF, the two western parties, ever came to play an important role in federal politics, though the CCF did have 28 Members of Parliament elected in 1945. The arrival of John Diefenbaker, the first Canadian prime minister from the West, only further marginalized the two parties. Under Diefenbaker, a true representative of the West (Saskatchewan), as well as under the leadership of his successor, Lester B. Pearson, who truly understood the need to give the provinces more powers, the demands of the West almost seemed a thing of the past. They came to the fore once

again, however, during the 1970s, when the oil crisis caused world markets to reel. Residents of oil-rich Alberta took particular offence at Prime Minister Trudeau's various attempts to weaken the provinces by imposing unpopular policies such as the transfer of control over natural resources to the federal government.

At the end of the 1970s, the oil boom, combined with an economic slowdown in Ontario and Québec, gave Alberta almost total employment and made it the province with the highest revenue per capita. This record performance cost Alberta some credibility when it came to its demands for larger control of its oil and gas. The split between the province and the federal government widened, and in the 1980 federal elections, the Liberal Party, the party ultimately brought to power, failed to elect any members of parliament from British Columbia or Alberta. The Liberals thus led the country until 1984 without any representation from these two provinces. The National Energy Program tabled by the Trudeau government was the straw that broke the camel's back as far as Albertans were concerned. Under this program, the federal government was to claim a greater and greater share of the price of Canadian oil and natural gas, leaving only a very marginal amount of the profits generated by the explosion of the world markets for the provinces and producers. Pierre Trudeau's Liberal government, which had led Canada almost continuously for 17 years, was succeeded by the Progressive Conservative government of Brian Mulroney, which did away with the much-hated National Energy Program.

AUTONOMIST AMBITIONS

Drawing on Western Canada's sense of alienation and the extreme right's disappointment with the weakness of the Mulroney government, Preston Manning, son of Ernest Manning (Prime Minister of Alberta from 1944 to 1968), founded the Reform Party in Vancouver in 1987. This party advocated, among other things, a smaller, less costly federal government and the reduction of federal expenditures. Westerners massively supported the Reform Party during the 1993 and 1997 elections.

Talk of British Columbia separating first surfaced in the late 1980s and has resurfaced many times since. As a province whose economic well-being is more dependent on Asia than on the rest of Canada, it is naturally less interested in what goes on in Ottawa. This is further emphasized by the fact that its industries are heavily based on the exploitation of natural resources, and that these are for the most part provincially regulated, except fisheries. And the feeling goes both ways; Ottawa is not involved in and therefore rarely spends much time on B.C. issues; its endless constitutional wrangling is that much more resented by British Columbians.

▲ John Diefenbaker pointing at an adversary in the House of Commons. © *Archives Canada; C-080883*

▲ Lester B. Pearson. © *Glenbow Archives; NA-1491-2*

Next page
▶ A typical mountain road in the Rockies.
© *iStockphoto.com / Jason Verschoor*

Vancouver

Vancouver ★ ★ ★ is truly a new city, one framed by the mighty elements of sea and mountains. Located in what was long one of the most isolated reaches on the planet, the city has, over the last 100 years, developed close ties with the nations of the largest ocean on Earth, and is one of the most multicultural metropolises of the Pacific Rim. Its history is tied to the development of British Columbia's natural resources. Most residents were lured here by the magnificent setting and the climate, which is remarkably mild in a country known for its bitter winters and stifling summers. Vancouver, where Asia meets America, is a city well worth discovering.

Pacific-minded though it is, Vancouver does not actually face right onto the ocean, but is separated from the sea by Vancouver Island, where Victoria, the capital of British Columbia, is located. Vancouver, the province's economic hub, lies on the Strait of Georgia, an arm of the sea separating Vancouver Island from the mainland. Its population is scattered across two peninsulas formed by Burrard Inlet to the north and False Creek to the south.

© Philippe Renault

Point Grey, the larger, more southerly peninsula, is home to the University of British Columbia and sprawling residential neighbourhoods. On the smaller peninsula to the north, visitors will discover a striking contrast between the east end, with its cluster of downtown skyscrapers, and the west end, occupied by the lovely, unspoiled woodlands of Stanley Park.

GASTOWN ★

At the end of the 19th century, rail transportation and the gold rush were driving the economic development of Gastown, which would become an important distribution centre for merchandise. Its warehouses were soon so full that a second "warehouse district" was created in Yaletown, which ended up supplanting Gastown. After a long decline, Gastown's restoration was undertaken in the middle of the 1960s and continues today.

Located a short walk from downtown and the Cruise Ship Terminal, Gastown is high on the agenda of many sightseers and cruise-ship passengers on a day pass. Today, Gastown is a historic district with many handsome late-19th and early 20th-century Victorian and Edwardian commercial vernacular buildings, which narrowly escaped the wrecker's ball in the late 1960s. Although many of these buildings now house good restaurants and popular

◄ A Vancouver landmark: the Gastown Steam Clock. © iStockphoto.com / Ronnie Comeau

◄ The attractive Gastown neighbourhood.
© Tourism Vancouver / Tom Ryan

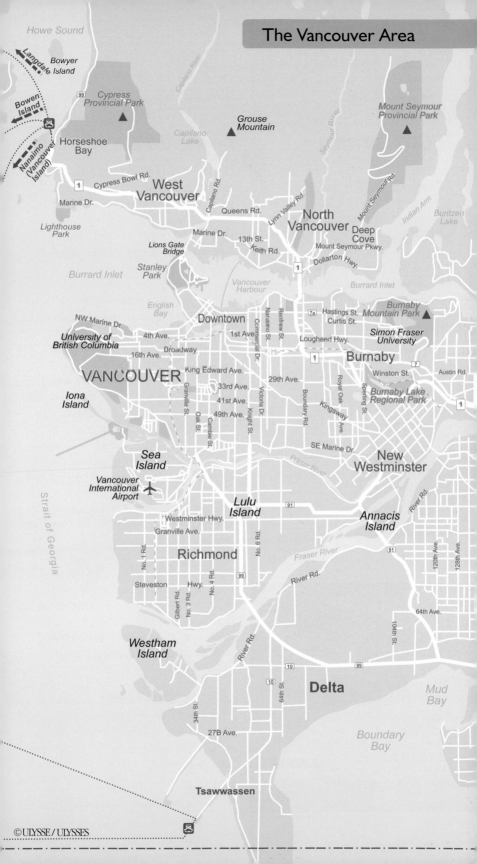

The Vancouver Area

Howe Sound

Langdale

Bowyer Island

Bowen Island

Nanaimo (Vancouver Island)

Cypress Provincial Park

Grouse Mountain

Mount Seymour Provincial Park

Horseshoe Bay

Capilano Lake

Capilano River

Seymour River

Indian Arm

Buntzen Lake

Cypress Bowl Rd.

West Vancouver

Marine Dr.

Queens Rd.

Lynn Valley Rd.

North Vancouver

Deep Cove

Mount Seymour Pkwy.

Lighthouse Park

Lions Gate Bridge

Marine Dr.

13th St.

Keith Rd.

Mount Seymour Rd.

Dollarton Hwy.

Burrard Inlet

Stanley Park

Vancouver Harbour

Burrard Inlet

English Bay

Downtown

Hastings St.

Curtis St.

Burnaby Mountain Park

NW Marine Dr.

4th Ave.

1st Avenue

Commercial Dr.

Renfrew St.

Nanaimo St.

Lougheed Hwy.

Simon Fraser University

University of British Columbia

Broadway

16th Ave.

King Edward Ave.

29th Ave.

Burnaby

Winston St.

Austin Rd.

VANCOUVER

33rd Ave.

41st Ave.

49th Ave.

Granville St.

Oak St.

Cambie St.

Knight St.

Victoria Dr.

Boundary Rd.

Royal Oak Ave.

Kingsway

Sperling St.

Burnaby Lake Regional Park

Iona Island

Sea Island

SE Marine Dr.

New Westminster

Vancouver International Airport

Strait of Georgia

Lulu Island

Westminster Hwy.

Granville Ave.

No. 1 Rd.

Richmond

Fraser River

Annacis Island

River Rd.

120th Ave.

128th Ave.

Steveston

Gilbert Rd.

No. 3 Rd.

No. 4 Rd.

Hwy.

No. 6 Rd.

Fraser River

River Rd.

104th St.

64th Ave.

Westham Island

River Rd.

Delta

Mud Bay

34th St.

64th St.

27B Ave.

Boundary Bay

Tsawwassen

©ULYSSE / ULYSSES

nightspots, the district has somehow managed to retain a whiff of that "Wild West" atmosphere.

to China. There are around 260,000 Canadian passport holders living in Hong Kong today.

CHINATOWN ★★

The 1858 Gold Rush in the hinterland drew Chinese from San Francisco and Hong Kong; in 1878, railway construction brought thousands more Chinese to British Columbia. This community resisted many hard blows that might have ended its presence in the province. At the beginning of the 20th century, the Canadian government imposed a heavy tax on new Chinese immigrants, and then banned Chinese immigration altogether from 1923 to 1947.

But while Vancouver's Chinatown is one of the largest in all of North America, much of Vancouver's Chinese population now lives in Richmond, south of Vancouver. After Great Britain returned Hong Kong to China in 1997, immigrants flocked to Vancouver. But 10 years later, the tide has turned, and some immigrants who made their fortune in Canada are now returning

DOWNTOWN ★★

On May 23, 1887, the first Canadian Pacific transcontinental train arrived from Montréal at the Vancouver terminus. The railway company, which had been granted an area roughly corresponding to present-day downtown Vancouver, began to develop its property. To say that it played a major role in the development of the city's business district would be an understatement. Canadian Pacific truly built this part of town, laying the streets and erecting many very important buildings. Downtown Vancouver has been developing continually since the 1960s. It's a sign of the city's great economic vitality, which can be attributed to Asian capital and Canadians moving westward to the mild climes of the Pacific coast.

The **Marine Building** ★★ is a fine example of the Art Deco style. It's characterized by vertical lines, staggered recesses, geometric ornamentation and the absence of a cornice at the top of the structure. Erected in 1929, the building lives up to its name in part because it is lavishly decorated with nautical motifs, and also because its occupants are ship-owners and shipping companies.

The **Provincial Law Courts** ★, designed by talented Vancouver architect Arthur Erickson, were completed in 1978. The vast interior space, accented in glass and steal, is worth a visit. The court-

◀ The gates of Chinatown. © *Philippe Renault*

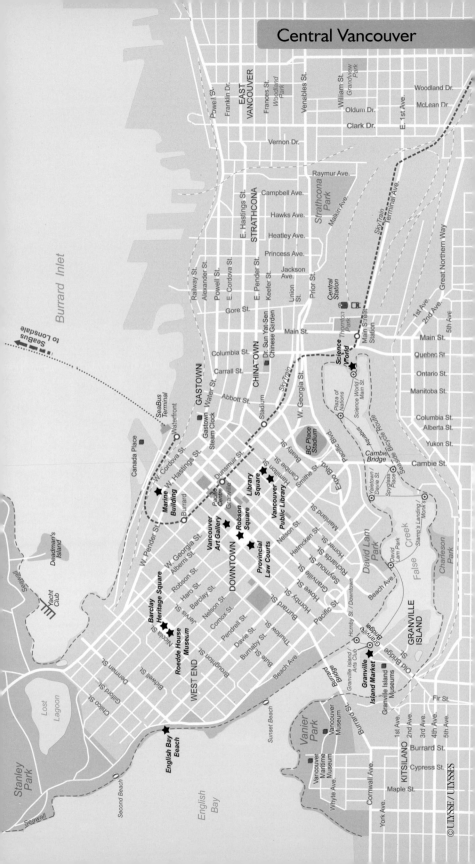

Central Vancouver

Burrard Inlet

SeaBus to Lonsdale

EAST VANCOUVER

STRATHCONA

Strathcona Park

Woodland Park

Woodland Dr.
McLean Dr.
Grandview Park
William St.
Oldum Dr.
Clark Dr.
E. 1st Ave

Franklin Dr.
Powell St.
Frances St.
Venables St.
Raymur Ave.
Campbell Ave.
Hawks Ave.
Heatley Ave.
Princess Ave.
Jackson Ave.
Keefer St.
Union St.
Prior St.

Vernon Dr.

E. Hastings St.
Railway St.
Alexander St.
Powell St.
E. Cordova St.
Gore St.
Columbia St.
Carrall St.
Abbott St.

GASTOWN

CHINATOWN

Dr. Sun Yat-Sen Chinese Garden

Main St.

Central Station
Thornton Park
Main Street Station

1st Ave.
2nd Ave.
Great Northern Way
Main St.
Quebec St.
Ontario St.
Manitoba St.
Columbia St.
Alberta St.
Yukon St.
Cambie St.

★ Science World
Science World / Main St.

Canada Place
SeaBus Terminal
Waterfront

W. Cordova St.
W. Hastings St.
Burrard

★ Marine Building

Gastown Steam Clock

Stadium
W. Georgia St.
W. Pender St.
Dunsmuir St.
Granville
Pacific Centre

★ Vancouver Art Gallery
★ Robson Square
★ Vancouver Public Library
Library Square
★ Provincial Law Courts

BC Place Stadium
Plaza of Nations
Pacific Blvd
Expo Blvd
Cambie Bridge

Yaletown / Davie St.
Spyglass Place
Stamp's Landing / Monk's
Seaside Bicycle Route
Cambie St.

Hamilton St.
Cambie St.
Beatty St.
Smithe St.
Nelson St.
Helmcken St.
Mainland St.
Homer St.
Richards St.
Seymour St.
Granville St.
Howe St.
Hornby St.
Burrard St.

DOWNTOWN

Alberni St.
W. Georgia St.
Robson St.
Haro St.
Barclay St.
Nelson St.
Comox St.
Pendrell St.
Davie St.
Burnaby St.
Beach Ave.

★ Barclay Heritage Square
★ Roedde House Museum

WEST END

Nicola St.
Jervis St.
Broughton St.
Bidwell St.
Cardero St.
Denman St.
Chilco St.
Gilford St.

Lost Lagoon

Stanley Park

Deadman's Island

Yacht Club
Seawall

Second Beach

Seawall

English Bay

★ English Bay Beach

Sunset Beach

David Lam Park
David Lam Park
False Creek
Charleson Park

GRANVILLE ISLAND

Granville Island / Arts Club
★ Granville Island Market
Granville Island Museums

Old Bridge St.
Granville Bridge
Burrard Bridge
Beach Ave.
Pacific Blvd
Hornby St. / Downtown
Granville / Downtown

Vanier Park
Vancouver Museum
Vancouver Maritime Museum

KITSILANO
Cornwall Ave.
Whyte Ave.
York Ave.
Maple St.
Cypress St.
Fir St.
Burrard St.
1st Ave
2nd Ave
3rd Ave
4th Ave
5th Ave

© ULYSSE / ULYSSES

DOWNTOWN EASTSIDE

The Downtown Eastside is defined by Burrard Inlet to the north, East Hastings Street to the south, Clark Drive to the east and Main Street to the west. Formerly a dynamic commercial and cultural area in the centre of Vancouver's business district, it experienced a downturn toward the end of the 1990s, after the 1993 closure of the Woodward's store led to the failure of a number of other nearby stores and businesses. It became Canada's poorest neighbourhood, and public disorder reigned: drug trafficking, prostitution, crime, drug addition and homelessness, not to mention AIDS and other calamities. In 1996, over 80% of its families were classified as "low income" by Statistics Canada, compared with 31% of families in Vancouver in general.

However, its handsome Victorian buildings testify to a once-vibrant neighbourhood. Vancouver's first downtown developed here in the early 20th century, near the nucleus of the growing city. It was home to the municipal courthouse, the city hall, the Carnegie Public Library, several theatres and Woodward's department store. It was also the transportation hub of the city, with the streetcar station located at Hastings and Carrall Streets, and the ferry and pier just north on Burrard Inlet.

Today, a number of community organizations work tirelessly to improve the lot of the area's residents. The 2002 election of mayor Larry Campbell, for whom the clean-up of the Downtown Eastside was a priority, was a clear sign that change was on the horizon. The Vancouver Agreement, a plan signed by all three levels of government in 2000, has for main objective to promote and support economic and social investments in the community. The plan, which runs to 2010, is a key factor in the city's Downtown Eastside Revitalization Program, a multi-faceted approach to restoring the area to a healthy, safe and liveable neighbourhood for all.

house and **Robson Square** ★★, by the same architect, form a lovely ensemble. Vancouver's luxuriant vegetation (sustained by abundant rainfall and a temperate climate), unlike anything else in Canada, is put to maximum use here. Plants are draped along rough concrete walls and in between multiple little stepped ponds over which little waterfalls flow. Shops, restaurants and a skating rink welcome passers-by.

The **Vancouver Art Gallery** ★, located north of Robson Square, occupies the former Provincial Law Courts. This big, sumptuous, neoclassical-style building was erected in 1908 according to a design by British architect Francis Mawson Rattenbury. His other credits include the British Columbia Legislative Assembly and the Empress Hotel, both located in Victoria on Vancouver Island. Later, Rattenbury returned to his native country and was murdered by his wife's lover. The building was renovated by Arthur Erickson in the 1980s. Painted gray and white and ornately decorated with bas-relief, its rotunda is quite simply magnificent.

The same can be said of the Emily Carr gallery on the fourth floor, decorated in the same style and fondly referred to by the staff as the "wedding cake room." The gallery is home to an important collection of more than 200 works by Emily Carr, most of which are paintings. Selections are displayed on a rotating basis. Emily Carr (1871-1945) was a major Canadian painter whose primary subjects were the Aboriginal peoples and landscapes of the West Coast. One look at her magnificent red cedars, vividly rendered with expressive swooshes of blue and green, reminds us why her work is so cherished by Westerners. The gallery also hosts very contemporary travelling exhibits, and there is a lovely café with a reasonably priced menu on site.

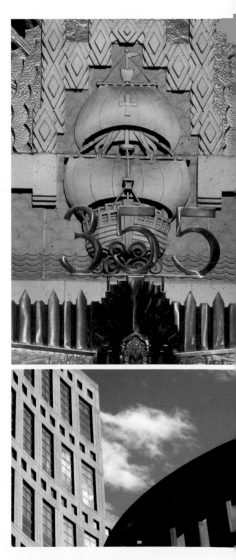

▲ Detail of the facade of the Marine Building.
© *Philippe Renault*

▶ The Vancouver Public Library recalls Rome's Coliseum. © *iStockphoto.com / Zubin Li*

Pages 34-35

◀ Aerial photo of Vancouver, the metropolis of Western Canada. © *iStockphoto.com / Kevin Miller*

KNOWING YOUR WEST END
FROM YOUR WEST SIDE

A first glance at any map of Vancouver can be a real brow-wrinkler. Just when you think you've figured out where the West End is, you're confronted with a West Side; then you realize that there's both an Eastside and an East Vancouver—not to mention three bodies of water surrounding the city! So, in the interest of smoothing out the wrinkles, here's a brief glance at Vancouver's geography.

Gastown is located in the northeastern corner of downtown, beginning at the intersection of Richards, Water and West Cordova streets, and stretching a few blocks east, roughly to Carrall Street. It is bounded to the south by West Cordova Street and to the north by Burrard Inlet.

Chinatown stretches southeast of Gastown, from Carrall Street in the west to Gore Street in the east, and from East Pender Street in the north to East Georgia Street in the south.

The **Downtown Eastside** is bounded by Burrard Inlet to the north and Hastings Street to the south, Clark Drive to the east and Main Street to the west.

▲ Modern Vancouver's dynamic skyline. © iStockphoto.com / Dan Barnes

East Vancouver, not to be confused with the Downtown Eastside, includes the area east of Ontario Street (south of False Creek) and is centred on Commercial Drive.

Downtown takes over where the West End leaves off and extends east to Main Street, on the north side of False Creek.

The **West End** stretches from Stanley Park in the west to Burrard Street in the east. Georgia Street is the northern boundary and English Bay the southern boundary. Beyond these areas is Vancouver's downtown.

Stanley Park is bounded by Burrard Inlet everywhere except to the east, where it is bounded by the West End.

Burrard Inlet separates North Vancouver and West Vancouver from the city of Vancouver.

False Creek separates the downtown area from the West Side, but three bridges—Burrard, Granville Street and Cambie—make the separation seem more psychological than geographical.

The **West Side**, not to be confused with the West End, is located south of False Creek. It includes everything west of Ontario Street, including the communities of Fairview and Kitsilano, as well as the University Endowment Lands.

At the corner of Robson and Homer streets is a curious building that is more than a little reminiscent of Rome's Coliseum—the **Vancouver Public Library ★★★**. This impressive building, completed in 1994-1995 and located on a city block known as **Library Square**, is the work of Montréal architect Moshe Safdie, known for his Habitat '67 in Montréal and the National Art Gallery in Ottawa. The project stirred lively reactions both from local people and from architecture critics. The design was chosen after finally being put to a referendum. The six-storey atrium is positively grandiose.

WEST END ★★

The population of the West End is a mixture of students and professionals, many of whom made a fortune on new technologies and the various new therapies now in fashion. The gay community is also well represented here.

Barclay Heritage Square is bounded by Barclay, Nicola, Haro and Broughton streets. There are eight heritage houses on this square, which is actually an Edwardian garden with its very own gazebo, all of which date from the 1890s. One of them has been reborn as a museum showcasing furnishings from the Victorian period. Built in 1893, the **Roedde House Museum ★★** was the family home of Gustav and Matilda Roedde and their family until 1925. Gustav was the first bookbinder and printer in Vancouver, a vocation profitable enough to permit the construction of a comfortable upper-middle-class home. The house was designed by notable architect and family friend

◄ The West End residential neighbourhood.
© *Pierre Longnus*

▼ English Bay. © *Pierre Longnus*

Francis Rattenbury. Ten of the home's 12 rooms are furnished with period pieces, most of which were donated to the museum by individuals; others are on loan from the Vancouver Museum and some are original to the house. The attention to detail is astounding and anyone with an interest with Victoriana and Art Nouveau will be delighted by this charming little museum.

The fine sands of **English Bay Beach** ★★ are always crowded during the summer. At the east end of the beach, visitors will find an enormous inukshuk created by Alvin Kanak for the Northwest Territories pavilion at Expo 86; it was moved to this site the following year. The apartment high-rises behind the beach give beach-goers the illusion that they are lounging about at a seaside resort like Acapulco, when they are actually just a short distance from the heart of Vancouver. Few cities can boast beaches so close to their downtown core. Fleets of sailboats skim across the magnificent bay, which has recently been cleaned of pollutants. To the west, it is bordered by the verdant expanse of Stanley Park.

▲ The Seawall in Stanley Park, a popular recreation spot. © iStockphoto.com / M. Gillespie

STANLEY PARK ★★★

Lord Stanley, for whom the National Hockey League's Stanley Cup was named, founded Stanley Park on a romantic impulse back in the 19th century when he was Canada's Governor General (1888-1893), and dedicated it "to the use and enjoyment of people of all colours, creeds and customs for all time." Like New York's Central Park and Montréal's Mount Royal, Stanley Park was largely designed by renowned landscape architect Frederick Law Olmsted.

Stanley Park lies on an elevated peninsula stretching into the Georgia Strait, and encompasses over 400ha of flowery gardens, dense woodlands and lookouts offering views of the sea and the mountains. Obviously Vancouver's many skyscrapers have not prevented the city from maintaining close ties with the nearby wilderness.

A 10km waterfront promenade known as the **Seawall** ★★ runs around the park, enabling pedestrians to drink in every bit of the stunning scenery here. The **Stanley Park Scenic Drive** is the

Stanley Park

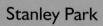
Stanley Park

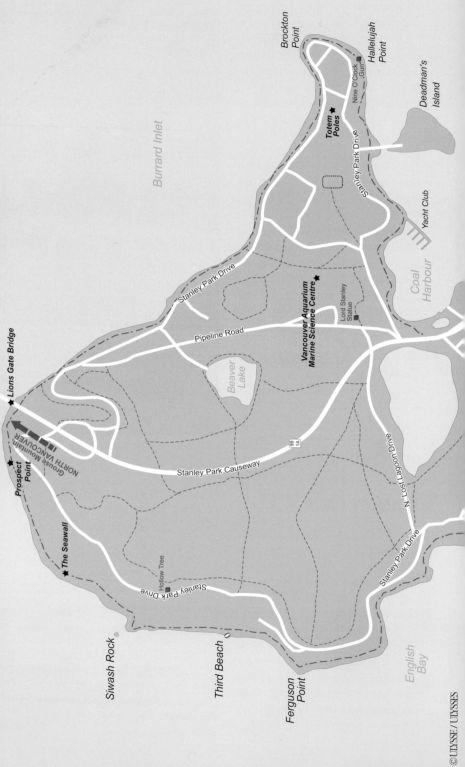

Brockton
Point

Hallelujah
Point

Nine O'Clock
Gun

Deadman's
Island

★ **Totem
Poles**

Stanley Park Drive

Yacht Club

Burrard Inlet

Coal
Harbour

Stanley Park Drive

Vancouver Aquarium
Marine Science Centre

Lord Stanley
Statue

Pipeline Road

Beaver
Lake

★ Lions Gate Bridge

99
1A

N. Lost Lagoon Drive

Grouse Mountain
NORTH VANCOUVER

★
Prospect
Point

Stanley Park Causeway

Stanley Park Drive

★ The Seawall

Hollow Tree

Stanley Park Drive

Siwash Rock

Third Beach

Ferguson
Point

English
Bay

© ULYSSE / ULYSSES

equivalent of the Seawall for motorists. This road runs one-way in a counter-clockwise direction.

The renowned **Vancouver Aquarium Marine Science Centre ★★★** is appropriately located by the ocean. It displays representatives of the marine animal life of the West Coast and the Pacific as a whole, including magnificent killer whales, belugas, dolphins and exotic fish.

The aquarium's outside exhibit is home to harbour seals, Spinnaker the dolphin, sea otters and belugas, all of which face particular challenges that prevent them from being released into the wild. Inside, there are underwater viewing areas for the belugas and dolphins. The *Treasures of the B.C. Coast* displays representative ecosystems, one tank for each area, complete with interpretive panels. There is a section on the shores of Stanley Park, supplied by seawater piped in from Burrard Inlet. Finally, the *Amazon* gallery, where rainforest

▲ Like a fish to water… © *Vancouver Aquarium*

▲ A totem pole in Stanley Park. © *iStockphoto.com*

Next pages

▶ Vancouver's Coal Harbour and Financial District. © *iStockphoto.com / Riaan de Beer*

residents of all kinds make their home, including sloths and free-flying Costa Rican butterflies, is another must-see.

Further east are the famous **Totem Poles ★** which are reminders of a sizeable Aboriginal population on the

Stanley Park

▲ The Seawall curves around Stanley Park. © *iStockphoto.com / Jennifer Oehler*

THE SEASIDE BICYCLE ROUTE

Among Vancouver's many bike paths, the most interesting one for visitors is undoubtedly the Seaside Bicycle Route. The route takes bike riders through some spectacular scenery along Burrard Inlet, Stanley Park, English Bay and False Creek.

Cyclists can pick up the trail on Burrard Inlet as far west as Thurlow Street, west of the Pan Pacific Hotel, and travel in a counterclockwise direction to Stanley Park, where they pick up the Seawall path. After riding the 10km Seawall, passing the totem poles, Lions Gate Bridge and several beaches, cyclists continue along English Bay to the shores of False Creek all the way to Science World. The route continues to Granville Island and along the shore of English Bay through to Vanier Park, Kitsilano Park and several beaches, ending at Spanish Bank West. Shortcuts can be taken from the north shore of False Creek to the south shore via the Cambie or Burrard bridges (the latter is a good bet for making a beeline to Granville Island). The entire route is about 30km long and is also part of the Trans Canada Trail. It's a fabulous way to experience Vancouver!

peninsula barely 150 years ago. Most of these totem poles, however, are fairly modern, having been carved since 1987. One was carved by famed Haida artist Bill Reid and his assistants in 1964.

Lions Gate Bridge ★★, an elegant suspension bridge built in 1938, is located some 2.5km further along the Seawall, past Brockton Point and some lovely landscapes. It spans the First Narrows, linking the affluent suburb of West Vancouver to the centre of town. At the entrance to the bridge, artist Charles Marega sculpted two immense lion heads. **Prospect Point ★★★**, to the west, offers a general view of the bridge, whose steel pillars stand 135m high.

BURRARD INLET ★★

Burrard Inlet is the long and very wide arm of the sea on which the Vancouver harbour—Canada's most important port for over 20 years now—is located. The Atlantic was once the favourite trading route, but the dramatic economic growth of the American West Coast (California, Oregon, Washington) and even more importantly, the Far East (Japan, Hong Kong, Taiwan, China, Singapore, Thailand, etc.), has crowned the Pacific Ocean lord and master of shipping.

In North Vancouver, at the north end of Nancy Greene Way, there is a cable car, the **Grouse Mountain Skyride**, that carries passengers to the top of **Grouse Mountain ★★★**. At an altitude of 1,250m, skiers and hikers can contemplate the entire Vancouver area as well as Washington State (in clear weather) to the south. The view is particularly beautiful at the end of the

▲ Lions Gate Bridge, a symbol of Vancouver.
© iStockphoto.com / Stephen Finn

day. Wilderness trails lead out from the various viewing areas. During summer, Grouse Mountain is also a popular spot for hang-gliding.

Also in the marvellous mountain range on the north shore, magnificent **Lynn Canyon Park ★★★** is scored with forest trails. It is best known for its footbridge, which stretches across an 80m deep gorge. Definitely not for the faint of heart! The park also hosts an ecology centre.

Mount Seymour Provincial Park ★★ is another good hiking locale, offering two different views of the region. To the east is Indian Arm, a large arm of the sea extending into the valley.

Burrard Inlet

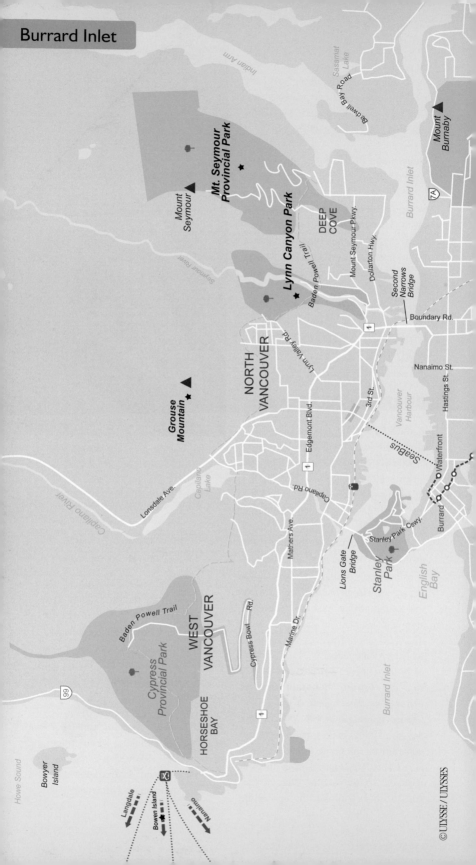

Burrard Inlet

Sasamat Lake

Indian Arm

Bedwell Bay Road

Mount Burnaby

Mt. Seymour Provincial Park

Mount Seymour

Lynn Canyon Park

DEEP COVE

Baden Powell Trail

Seymour River

Mount Seymour Pkwy.

Dollarton Hwy.

Second Narrows Bridge

Boundary Rd.

Nanaimo St.

Hastings St.

NORTH VANCOUVER

Lynn Valley Rd.

3rd St.

Vancouver Harbour

SeaBus

Grouse Mountain

Edgemont Blvd.

Capilano Rd.

Waterfront

Capilano Lake

Burrard

Lonsdale Ave.

Capilano River

Stanley Park Cswy.

Stanley Park

English Bay

Mathers Ave.

Lions Gate Bridge

Howe Sound

Baden Powell Trail

WEST VANCOUVER

Cypress Bowl Rd.

Marine Dr.

Burrard Inlet

Cypress Provincial Park

HORSESHOE BAY

Bowyer Island

Langdale

Bowen Island

Nanaimo

© ULYSSE / ULYSSES

50

A 15min ferry ride from Horseshoe Bay leads to **Bowen Island** ★★★, where hiking trails lead through a lush forest. Although it feels like you're at the other end of the world here, downtown Vancouver is only 5km away as the crow flies.

FALSE CREEK ★★

False Creek is located south of downtown Vancouver and, like Burrard Inlet, stretches far inland. The presence of both water and a railroad induced a large number of sawmills to set up shop in this area in the early 20th century. These mills gradually filled in a portion of False Creek, leaving only a narrow channel to provide them with the water needed for sawing. Over the

▶ One of the lovely waterfalls of Lynn Canyon Park. © *Pierre Longnus*

▼ The aerial tramway to the summit of Grouse Mountain. © *iStockphoto.com / Dave Logan*

IN MEMORIAM

To commemorate the December 6, 1989 shooting of 14 young women at the École Polytechnique de Montréal, the Women's Monument Committee unveiled a monument entitled *Marker of Change* on the eighth anniversary of the tragic event in 1997. Created by Torontonian Beth Alber and erected in Thornton Park, near the train and bus station, it features 14 pink granite benches laid out in a circle, each one bearing the name of one of the victims of the massacre. The monument's dedication, in honour of all women murdered by men, is written in seven languages.

years, two thirds of False Creek, as explorer George Vancouver had known it in 1790, has disappeared under asphalt.

By the early 1980s, the sawmills and other industries had disappeared and a century's worth of industrial pollution had left the area a mess. The City purchased the site, quickly cleaned it up, and during the summer of 1986 hosted Expo 86, a world's fair that attracted several million visitors in the space of a few months. The vast stretch of unused land along the north shore of False Creek was occupied by dozens of showy pavilions with visitors crowding around them. The City then rezoned the land for residential and commercial use and sold it to a Hong Kong tycoon for $145 million. At the end of False Creek is the large silver sphere that houses **Science World** ★, the only Expo 86 pavilion built to remain in place after the big event.

The industrial area of **Yaletown** ★★ developed in 1887 when the western terminal of the Canadian Pacific Railroad (CPR) was moved from Port Moody to Vancouver. The growth of

◀ The dome of Science World, formerly an Expo 86 pavilion. © iStockphoto.com / Dan Barnes

▶ The modern towers of the False Creek neighbourhood. © iStockphoto.com / Kevin Miller

A 15min ferry ride from Horseshoe Bay leads to **Bowen Island** ★★★, where hiking trails lead through a lush forest. Although it feels like you're at the other end of the world here, downtown Vancouver is only 5km away as the crow flies.

FALSE CREEK ★★

False Creek is located south of downtown Vancouver and, like Burrard Inlet, stretches far inland. The presence of both water and a railroad induced a large number of sawmills to set up shop in this area in the early 20th century. These mills gradually filled in a portion of False Creek, leaving only a narrow channel to provide them with the water needed for sawing. Over the

▶ One of the lovely waterfalls of Lynn Canyon Park. © *Pierre Longnus*

▼ The aerial tramway to the summit of Grouse Mountain. © *iStockphoto.com / Dave Logan*

IN MEMORIAM

To commemorate the December 6, 1989 shooting of 14 young women at the École Polytechnique de Montréal, the Women's Monument Committee unveiled a monument entitled *Marker of Change* on the eighth anniversary of the tragic event in 1997. Created by Torontonian Beth Alber and erected in Thornton Park, near the train and bus station, it features 14 pink granite benches laid out in a circle, each one bearing the name of one of the victims of the massacre. The monument's dedication, in honour of all women murdered by men, is written in seven languages.

years, two thirds of False Creek, as explorer George Vancouver had known it in 1790, has disappeared under asphalt.

By the early 1980s, the sawmills and other industries had disappeared and a century's worth of industrial pollution had left the area a mess. The City purchased the site, quickly cleaned it up, and during the summer of 1986 hosted Expo 86, a world's fair that attracted several million visitors in the space of a few months. The vast stretch of unused land along the north shore of False Creek was occupied by dozens of showy pavilions with visitors crowding around them. The City then rezoned the land for residential and commercial use and sold it to a Hong Kong tycoon for $145 million. At the end of False Creek is the large silver sphere that houses **Science World** ★, the only Expo 86 pavilion built to remain in place after the big event.

The industrial area of **Yaletown** ★★ developed in 1887 when the western terminal of the Canadian Pacific Railroad (CPR) was moved from Port Moody to Vancouver. The growth of

◀   The dome of Science World, formerly an Expo 86 pavilion. © iStockphoto.com / Dan Barnes

▶   The modern towers of the False Creek neighbourhood. © iStockphoto.com / Kevin Miller

VANCOUVER HOSTS THE 2010 OLYMPIC WINTER GAMES

Vancouver, the metropolis of British Columbia has been chosen by the International Olympic Committee (IOC) to host the XXI Olympic Winter Games in 2010. The other three finalist cities were Bern (Switzerland), Pyeongchang (South Korea) and Salzburg (Austria). The Winter Games will be held from February 12 to 28, 2010.

Within Vancouver, hockey games will be played at GM Place; curling competitions will take place in Hillcrest Park's new curling centre; figure skating and speed skating events will be held at Hastings Park's renovated Pacific Coliseum; and Vancouver's Olympic village will welcome athletes in Southeast False Creek.

Outside Vancouver, freestyle skiing and snowboarding competitions will take place in the renovated facilities at Cypress Mountain; other hockey games will be held at the University of British Columbia's new winter stadium; Richmond's new ice rink will host the long track speed skating meets; alpine skiing (downhill, slalom and combined events) will be held at the renovated facilities at Whistler Creekside and Whistler Blackcomb; nordic skiing competitions (biathlon, cross-country, ski jumping and nordic combined) will take place at the Whistler Nordic Centre's new facilities (which will be built in the Callaghan Valley); bobsleigh, luge and skeleton events will be held at the new Whistler Sliding Centre, located on Blackcomb Mountain; and, finally, Whistler's athletes' village will also be located in the Callaghan Valley.

▲ Olympic luge. © viewcalgary.com

the trucking industry eventually shifted business away from Yaletown's big warehouses and the area declined, until a new group of tenants including designers, artists, and adventurous business people brought the area back to life during the 1990s. Today, it is one of Vancouver's trendiest and poshest neighbourhoods.

Located at the mouth of False Creek, **Granville Island ★★** was created in 1914 for industrial purposes. In 1977, the artificial island's warehouses and factories were transformed into a major recreational and commercial centre. The **Granville Island Market ★★★** is a definite must-see. The market is a feast for all the senses: there are stalls of oriental orchids, fishmongers with salmon in every shade of red, *focaccia* and fig-and-anise loaves at the wonderful Terra Breads, tempting Indian candy, bowls of smoked-salmon chowder at Stock Market, and atmosphere to spare.

WEST SIDE ★★★

The posh residential neighbourhoods of Kitsilano and West Point Grey, numerous museums, the University of British Columbia (UBC) campus and several sand and quartz beaches, from which Vancouver Island is visible on a clear day, make Vancouver's West Side a lively and enjoyable area.

The **Vancouver Museum ★★** stands in the heart of Vanier Park. This delightful museum, whose dome resembles the head-dress worn by members of the Coast Salish First Nation, presents

▼　A stroll along Kitsilano Beach. © *iStockphoto.com / Sigrid Albert*

exhibitions on the history of the different peoples who have inhabited the region.

The museum's Orientation Gallery boasts an eclectic collection, including items from all over the world amassed by Vancouverites and a photograph of Engine 374, which pulled the first transcontinental train into Vancouver, on May 23, 1887. Children love this gallery, which features a collection of toys, thoughtfully displayed in child-height glass exhibit cases. Finally, the museum offers some wonderful views of the West End and Stanley Park.

Vancouverites are proud of the beaches and parks that border English Bay: **Kitsilano Beach ★** is the perfect spot for a relaxing day in the sun; **Jericho Beach Park ★★** encompasses both a vast green space and a beach; **Spanish Banks Beach ★★** offers a breathtaking view of Vancouver and the north shore,

◀ Jericho Beach Park. © iStockphoto.com / Anthony Rosenberg

▼ Totem poles in the Museum of Anthropology. © UBC Museum of Anthropology / Bill McLennan

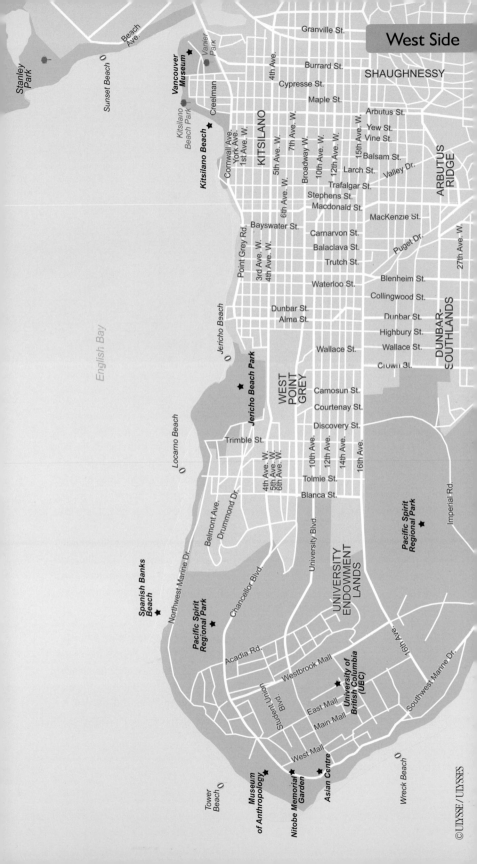

Granville St.

Burrard St.

SHAUGHNESSY

4th Ave.

Cypresse St.

Maple St.

Beach Ave.

Arbutus St.

Sunset Beach

Yew St.

Vine St.

Vanier Park

Vancouver Museum

4th Ave.

7th Ave. W.

15th Ave. W.

Balsam St.

ARBUTUS RIDGE

Stanley Park

Creelman

Kitsilano Beach Park

KITSILANO

Broadway W.

10th Ave. W.

12th Ave. W.

Larch St.

Valley Dr.

Kitsilano Beach

Cornwall Ave.

York Ave.

1st Ave. W.

5th Ave. W.

6th Ave. W.

Trafalgar St.

Stephens St.

Macdonald St.

MacKenzie St.

27th Ave. W.

Bayswater St.

Carnarvon St.

Point Grey Rd.

Balaclava St.

Puget Dr.

Trutch St.

3rd Ave. W.

4th Ave. W.

Waterloo St.

Blenheim St.

English Bay

Jericho Bsach

Dunbar St.

Alma St.

Collingwood St.

Dunbar St.

Highbury St.

DUNBAR-SOUTHLANDS

Jericho Beach Park

WEST POINT GREY

Wallace St.

Wallace St.

Crown St.

Locarno Beach

Camosun St.

Courtenay St.

Trimble St.

Discovery St.

4th Ave. W.

5th Ave. W.

6th Ave. W.

10th Ave.

12th Ave.

14th Ave.

16th Ave.

Tolmie St.

Blanca St.

Pacific Spirit Regional Park

Belmont Ave.

Drummond Dr.

University Blvd.

Imperial Rd.

Spanish Banks Beach

Chancellor Blvd.

UNIVERSITY ENDOWMENT LANDS

Pacific Spirit Regional Park

Northwest Marine Dr.

16th Ave.

Acadia Rd.

Westbrook Mall

Southwest Marine Dr.

Student Union Blvd.

University of British Columbia (UBC)

East Mall

Main Mall

Wreck Beach

West Mall

Tower Beach

Museum of Anthropology

Nitobe Memorial Garden

Asian Centre

▲ Nitobe Memorial Garden, a beautiful Japanese garden. © *iStockphoto.com / Karen Massier*

particularly at sunset; finally, **Pacific Spirit Regional Park ★★** is a 763ha parcel of land that boasts more than 40km of hiking and biking trails.

The **University of British Columbia (UBC) ★★** has occupied the West Side's westernmost tip area since 1925. To this day, the UBC campus is constantly expanding, so its somewhat heterogeneous appearance should not be surprising. The campus is home to the superb **Museum of Anthropology ★★★**, which is not to be missed both for the quality of the Aboriginal artwork on display and for the architecture of Arthur Erickson. Erickson designed the Great Hall with big concrete posts and beams to imitate the shape of traditional Aboriginal houses. Inside are immense totem poles gathered from former Aboriginal villages along the coast and on the islands.

A highlight of the museum is the sculpture *Raven and the First Men* by renowned Haida artist Bill Reid, who died in 1998. This impressive yellow cedar piece depicts the Raven, an infamous trickster in Haida history, coaxing fearful human beings out of a clam shell after a great flood. This huge piece was lowered into the museum through the skylight above it. The museum's outdoor exhibit, a 19th-century Haida house complex, is another must-see.

On the edge of the West Mall is the **Asian Centre**, capped with a big pyramidal metal roof. It houses the department of Asian studies and an exhibition centre. Behind the building is the magnificent **Nitobe Memorial Garden ★★** which symbolically faces Japan on the other side of the Pacific.

West Side

Victoria and Surroundings

Is **Victoria** ★ ★ ★ really more English than England? Immigrants loyal to the British Crown who chose this city to start their lives over brought with them some of their customs and habits, giving Victoria its characteristic British cachet. This is still a North American city, however, and along with all the English, it has welcomed large numbers of Chinese, Japanese, Scots, Irish, Germans, French Canadians and Americans.

Located at the southern tip of Vancouver Island, Victoria is the capital of British Columbia and has a population of nearly 350,000 scattered across a large urban area. Its harbour looks out onto the Strait of Juan de Fuca, a natural border with Washington State. Victoria is set against a series of small mountains no higher than 300m in altitude, and its waterfront stretches several kilometres.

The downtown area rises up behind the port, whose waters are shared by ships, yachts and ferries. Like a railway station surrounded by yards, the port is the focal point; the squares, hotels, museums and parliament buildings are

© iStockphoto.com / S. Greg Panosian

all located nearby. A stroll along the waterfront gives a good sense of how the city has preserved a human dimension in its squares and streets.

INNER HARBOUR AND OLD TOWN ★ ★ ★

Any tour of Victoria starts at the **Inner Harbour**, which was the main point of access into the city for decades. Back in the era of tall ships, the merchant marine operating on the Pacific Ocean used to stop here to pick up goods destined for England.

Now owned by the Fairmont chain of hotels, the **Empress Hotel** ★ ★ was built in 1905 for the Canadian Pacific Railway company. It was designed by Francis Rattenbury in the Chateau style, just like the Chateau Frontenac in Québec City, only more modern and less romantic. A stroll through the main lobby transports visitors back to the 1920s, when the names of influential people found their way into the hotel's guest books, and any trip to Victoria should include a stop by the Empress for afternoon tea.

▼ The Inner Harbour and old Victoria at dusk. © iStockphoto.com / Andrew Penner

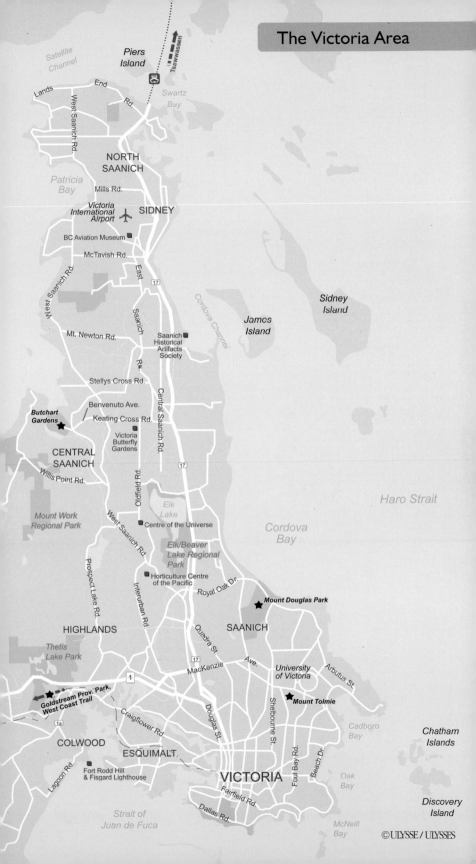

The Victoria Area

Satellite
Channel

*Piers
Island*

Teawwassen

Lands — End — Rd.

*Swartz
Bay*

West Saanich Rd.

**NORTH
SAANICH**

*Patricia
Bay*

Mills Rd.

Victoria
International
Airport

SIDNEY

BC Aviation Museum

McTavish Rd.

East

West Saanich Rd.

17

Cordova Channel

*Sidney
Island*

Mt. Newton Rd.

Saanich

*James
Island*

Saanich
Historical
Artifacts
Society

Stellys Cross Rd.

Rd.

Central Saanich Rd.

Benvenuto Ave.

***Butchart
Gardens***

Keating Cross Rd.

Victoria
Butterfly
Gardens

**CENTRAL
SAANICH**

Willis Point Rd.

17

Oldfield Rd.

*Elk
Lake*

West Saanich Rd.

Centre of the Universe

*Mount Work
Regional Park*

*Cordova
Bay*

Haro Strait

*Elk/Beaver
Lake Regional
Park*

Prospect Lake Rd.

Interurban Rd.

Horticulture Centre
of the Pacific

Royal Oak Dr.

HIGHLANDS

*Thetis
Lake Park*

Mount Douglas Park

SAANICH

Quadra St.

17

MacKenzie

Ave.

University
of Victoria

Arbutus St.

1

Goldstream Prov. Park,
West Coast Trail

Mount Tolmie

Shelbourne St.

1a

Craigflower Rd.

Douglas St.

*Cadboro
Bay*

*Chatham
Islands*

COLWOOD

ESQUIMALT

Lagoon Rd.

Fort Rodd Hill
& Fisgard Lighthouse

VICTORIA

Foul Bay Rd.

Beach Dr.

*Oak
Bay*

*Discovery
Island*

Fairfield Rd.

Dallas Rd.

*Strait of
Juan de Fuca*

*McNeill
Bay*

©ULYSSE / ULYSSES

Central Victoria

Oak Bay

Uplands Park

Oak Bay Marina

Victoria Golf Club

Anderson Hill Park

Beach Dr.

McNeil Bay

Dorset Rd.

Burdick Ave.
Burdick Ave.
Dufferin Ave.
Musgrave St.
Thompson Ave.
Cavendish Ave.
Bower Ave.
Cranmore Rd.
Dalhousie St.

Newport Ave.
Linkleas Ave.
Byng St.
Island Rd.
Transit Rd.
St Patrick St.
Oliver St.

Henderson Rd.

Camarvon Park

Beach Dr.
Newport Ave.
Currie Rd.
Orchard Ave.
Windsor Park

Hampshire Rd.

Windsor Rd.

Monterey Ave.
Hampshire Rd.
Victoria Ave.
Falkland Rd.

McNeil Ave.
Central Ave.
Beach Dr.

Crescent Rd.

Gonzales Bay

Foul Bay Rd.

OAK BAY

Leighton Rd.

Oak Bay Ave.

Brighton Ave.

Clawthorn St.

Foul Bay Rd.

Lillian St.
Beechwood Ave.
Wildwood Ave.

Taylor St.
Neil St.
Allenby St.
Townley St.
Camarvon St.
Newton St.
Kings Rd.
Haultain St.

Richmond Ave.

Fort St.

Rockland Ave

St Charles St.

Gonzales Ave.
Richmond Ave.
Richardson St.
Chandler Ave.

Ross Bay

Shelbourne St.

Scott St.
Ryan St.
Victor St.
Forbes St.
Belmont Ave.
Asquith St.
Avebury Ave.
Roseberry Ave.

Myrtle Ave.
Pearl St.

Cedar Hill Rd.

Denman St.
Pembroke St.
Gladstone Ave.
Vining St.
Stanley Ave.

Begbie St.

Gouvernment House

St Charles St.

ROCKLAND

Moss St.

Joseph St.
Olive St.
Moss St.
Howe St.
Wellington Ave.
Linden Ave.
Faithful St.

St Kguina

Ross Bay Cemetery

Ross Bay

Walnut St.
Femwood Rd.

Grant St.
Balmoral Rd.

Craigdarroch Castle

Art Gallery of Greater Victoria

Fairfield Rd.

Moss St.

Kings Rd.
Topaz Ave.
Vista Heights

Empress Ave.

Park St.
Caledonia Ave.
Vancouver St.

Rudin St.

Linden Ave.

Cook St.

Johnson St.
Yates St.
View St.

Meares St.
Rockland Ave.
Burdett Ave.

Richardson St.
Collinson St.

Oscar St.
McKenzie St.
Oxford St.
Chapman St.
May St.

Central Park

Royal Athletic Park

Quadra St.

Pandora Av.

Blanshard St.

Courtney St.

Crystal Garden

Humboldt St.
Southgate St.

Vancouver St.
Heywood Ave.

Arbulus Way

Circle Dr.

Beacon Hill Park

Topaz Park

Hillside Av.

Bay St.

Queens Ave.
Princess Ave.
Pembroke St.
Discovery St.
Chatham St.
Herald St.
Fisgard St.

Government St.

Fort St.
Broughton St.

Royal BC Museum

Carr House

Dallas Rd.

17

Wharf St.

Empress Hotel

Legislature Building

JAMES BAY

Manchester St.
Dunedin St.
Garbally Rd.
Ellice St.
David St.
Hillside Ave.
John St.

Bridge St.
Turner St.
Pleasant St.

Belleville St.
Quebec St.

Superior St.
Michigan St.
Montreal St.
Ontario St.
Simcoe St.

St Lawrence St.

Oswego St.
MacDonald Park

Niagara St.
Menzies St.

Turner St.

Dallas Rd.

Holland Point Park

Dock St.
Pilot St.

Gorge Rd.
1A

Upper Harbour

Harbour Rd.

Tyee Rd.
Kimta Rd.

Victoria West Park

Esquimalt Rd.

Inner Harbour

Fisherman's Wharf

Raynor Ave.
Ashton St.
Catherine St.
Mary St.

Skinner St.
Bay St.

Barnfield Park

Russell St.

Victoria Harbour

Port Angeles

Strait of Juan de Fuca

ESQUIMALT

Seaforth Ave.
Craigflower Rd.
Colville St.

Langford St.
Wilson St.
Hereward Rd.

Pine St.
Carrie St.
Devonshire St.
Ellery St.
Old Esquimalt Rd.
Dunsmuir Rd.

Victoria View Rd.

© ULYSSE / ULYSSES

▲   The totem poles of the Royal BC
     Museum. © *Royal BC Museum*

▶   The Royal BC Museum's mammoth.
     © *Royal BC Museum*

The **Royal British Columbia Museum** ★★★ provides an overview of the history of the city and the various peoples that have inhabited the province. The spectacular *First Peoples* exhibit begins with historical artifacts juxtaposed alongside some contemporary art, like that of Musqueam artist Susan Point, to demonstrate the roots and evolution of Northwest Coast art of the type that can be found in the region's galleries, hotels and restaurants. Throughout the exhibit, there are clear distinctions between coastal and interior peoples and pre- and post-contact periods.

There is a wonderful exhibit of masks and totem poles, arranged by cultural group, with their distinctive elements identified. For example, visitors learn that Haida art is characterized by a carved, raised eyelid line and a concave orbit from the bridge of the nose to the temple to the nostril. There are also enormous feast dishes shaped like bears and wolves; magnificent Coast Salish capes, blankets and bags woven with cedar bark; a sound-and-light show explaining the cosmology of Northwest Coast First Nations; more than 100 Haida argillite carvings; and countless other items of interest.

In the *Modern History* exhibit, there are recreations of scenes from the last century of B.C.'s history, including a 1920s

▲ A nighttime view of the port of Victoria.
© *iStockphoto.com / Photo Service*

◄ The houseboats of tranquil Fisherman's Wharf. © *iStockphoto.com / Solidago*

◄ The provincial capital, Victoria, with its Parliament Buildings. © *iStockphoto.com / Jamey Ekins*

AFTERNOON TEA IN VICTORIA

The afternoon tea custom is one of the many ways in which Victoria's British heritage finds expression today. While known to China for 5,000 years, tea was introduced to the English court in the 17th century, but did not catch on for another two centuries or so.

The story goes that in the 1840s, Anna, the seventh Duchess of Bedford, got too hungry by mid-afternoon to wait until dinner time, commonly not much earlier than 9pm. So she ordered a snack of cakes, tarts, cookies, bread and butter, and tea to be brought to her boudoir. It wasn't long before the custom made its way into the drawing rooms of London, becoming a popular Victorian social custom among women of the privileged class.

By this time, the British East India Company was establishing tea plantations in Assam and other parts of India and Ceylon (Sri Lanka). The first shipment of Indian tea reached London in 1838.

Tea rooms as we now know them did not appear before 1864, when the enterprising manager of a bread shop near London Bridge began serving tea and snacks to her favourite clients.

Although there are a number of lovely tea rooms in Victoria, none has the cachet or genteel atmosphere of the Fairmont Empress Hotel's afternoon tea, which includes, in addition to a pot of Empress blend tea, delicate sandwiches, fresh scones with Jersey cream and strawberry jam, and light pastries.

▼   The Empress Hotel, Victoria's grand British-style hotel. © iStockphoto.com / Eric Hood

rococo-style theatre showing silent films; facades of Victorian buildings, including a hotel you can walk right into, its woodwork salvaged from a Nanaimo hotel; and a Chinatown street scene. The presentation is attractive and entertaining enough to keep children enthralled. There is also a *Natural History* exhibit, with models of different landscapes and ecosystems, the National Geographic Imax Theatre, and fascinating pools with local marine animals.

SCENIC MARINE DRIVE ★ ★

This fabulous scenic coastal road, at the bottom of the Saanich Peninsula, leads to a number of important Victoria attractions located inland. It passes through the communities of Fairfield, Rockland and Oak Bay.

The wooden **Carr House** ★ was erected in 1864 for the family of Richard Carr, but today it is mainly dedicated to the life of his daughter, the celebrated painter Emily Carr. Maps of the neighbourhood, which show where the family lived at various times, can also be obtained here. The only original piece of furniture in the house is the bed in which Emily was born in 1871, but it is nevertheless furnished in a style typical of the period. There is a small gift shop on site and a garden, animated by excerpts from Carr's writings.

Beacon Hill Park ★ is a peaceful spot where Emily Carr spent many happy days drawing. A public park laid out in 1890, it features a number of trails leading through fields of wildflowers and landscaped sections, as well as what is rumoured to be the world's tallest totem pole. The ebb and flow of the tides have transformed the park's shore into a pebble beach covered with pieces of driftwood.

Further North, the summit of **Mount Tolmie** ★ ★ ★ offers breathtaking panoramic views of Victoria, Haro Strait, the ocean, and magnificent Mount Baker and the Cascade Range in Washington State (U.S.A.).

SAANICH PENINSULA ★

Victoria lies at the southern end of the Saanich Peninsula. The peninsula is first and foremost a suburb, as many people who work in Victoria live here.

This region is an unavoidable part of any itinerary involving Vancouver Island and especially Victoria, since the big Swartz Bay Ferry Terminal is located in Sidney, a small town near the tip of the peninsula, accessed via the Patricia Bay Highway.

◄ A pretty garden and fountain in Beacon Hill Park. © iStockphoto.com / Sally Scott

▶ Carr House, birthplace of painter Emily Carr. © Parks Canada / Barrett & MacKay

EMILY CARR

After the American gold rush, Richard Carr and his family, who had been living in California, went home to their native England before returning to North America to set up residence in Victoria. Mr. Carr made a fortune in real estate and owned many pieces of land, both developed and undeveloped, in the James Bay residential area of Victoria. He died in 1888, having outlived his wife by two years. His daughter Emily was only 17 at the time. Shortly after, she went to San Francisco, London and finally Paris to study art.

She returned to British Columbia around 1910 and began teaching art to the children of Vancouver. She eventually went back to Victoria and followed in her father's footsteps, entering the real estate business. She also began travelling along the coast to paint, producing her greatest works in the 1930s.

A unique painter and a reclusive woman, Emily Carr is recognized across Canada as a great artist who left a unique stamp on the art world. While the Art Gallery of Greater Victoria features a few of her paintings, the Vancouver Art Gallery boasts the largest collection of her works.

On Vancouver's Granville Island, an institute dedicated to visual arts and design bears her name.

▲ The rose arches of Butchart Gardens. © *Butchart Gardens Ltd, Victoria, BC*

Mount Douglas Park ★★, which covers 10ha and offers access to the sea, is the perfect place for a picnic or a stroll. Its summit lookout offers a 360° view of the Southern Gulf Islands, the Strait of Georgia, the Strait of Juan de Fuca and the snow-capped peaks along the Canadian and U.S. coast. The colours of the sea and the mountains are most vibrant early in the morning and at the end of the day.

West Saanich Road

The **Butchart Gardens** ★★, which cover 26ha, were founded by the family of the same name in 1904. A wide array of flowers, shrubs and trees flourish in this unique space. A map is available at the entrance. During Summer, fireworks light up the sky on Saturday nights, and outdoor concerts are held here every evening.

Saanich Peninsula

THE TRANS-CANADA HIGHWAY

Kilometre zero of the Trans-Canada Highway (TCH), the longest national highway in the world, is indicated by a monument at the corner of Dallas Road and Douglas Street in Victoria. The TCH ends (or begins, depending on your point of view) 7,821 km to the east, in St. John's, in the province of Newfoundland and Labrador. In fact, in front of the St. John's city hall, a sign marking the spot declares that *"Canada begins right here…"*

Construction of the TCH began in the summer of 1950, and by the time it was completed in 1970 (the opening ceremonies took place in Rogers Pass, B.C. prior to completion, in 1962), it had cost $1 billion, more than three times the initial estimated cost.

In truth, the highway is neither a single entity, nor does it link the entire country. It needs some help from two ferries (from the mainland to Victoria and St. John's), doesn't quite manage to pass through every Canadian jurisdiction (the Yukon, Northwest Territories and Nunavut are left out), and is in fact two different highways for much of Ontario and Québec. West of Portage la Prairie, Manitoba, it splits into Highway 16, which heads north and ends up in Prince Rupert, B.C., and Highway 1, a southern route that ends up in Victoria.

The TCH's distinctive marker shield features a white maple leaf on a green background.

▼   Outside the city, delightful views line the highways. © *iStockphoto.com / Marek Slusarczyk*

Victoria to the West Coast Trail

◀   The lush temperate rainforest along the West
Coast Trail. © *Tourism Vancouver Island*

boasts 600-year-old Douglas firs lining hiking trails leading to Mount Finlayson and past magnificent waterfalls. From mid-October to early December, nature lovers come here during the **Salmon Run** to watch coho, chinook and chum salmon make their final voyage, spawn and die in Goldstream River. The fish are easy to see, as the water is crystal clear.

Port Renfrew

Port Renfrew is one of two starting points for the **West Coast Trail ★ ★ ★**. This five- to seven-day 75km trek is geared towards experienced, intrepid hikers prepared to face unstable weather conditions and widely varied terrain; in fact, it is considered one of the most difficult hiking trails in North America. This trail is part of the **Pacific Rim National Park Reserve**, an incredible green space divided into three areas: Long Beach, the Broken Group Islands and the West Coast Trail.

Further along after Port Renfrew, **Botanical Beach ★ ★ ★** is a veritable paradise for anyone interested in marine life. When the tide is out, little pools of water containing fish, starfish and various species of marine plant life are left behind among the pebbles.

FROM VICTORIA TO THE WEST COAST TRAIL ★ ★

Goldstream Provincial Park ★ ★

Located 16km west of Victoria, Goldstream Provincial Park is one of the major parks in the Victoria area. It

Vancouver Island and the Southern Gulf Islands

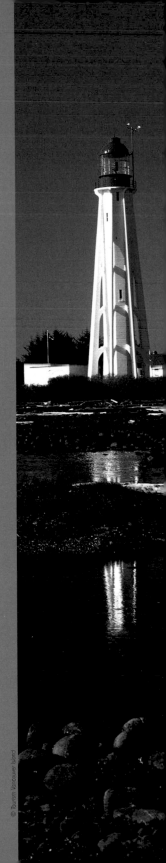

Vast Vancouver Island stretches over 500km along the West Coast, with its southern tip facing the Olympic Mountains in Washington State (U.S.A.). The island is split into two distinct regions by a chain of mountains that divides the north from the south. The sea has sculpted the island's west side, creating big, deep fjords; the shoreline on the east side is much smoother. Most of the towns and villages on the island lie along the Strait of Georgia, where the Southern Gulf Islands are located. The Northern Gulf Islands are clustered in the Johnstone Strait, northeast of Vancouver Island.

The forest and fishing industries have provided several generations with a good source of income in this magnificent region. Thanks to the warm currents of the Pacific, the climate is mild all year round, enhancing the quality of life here. Once isolated from the mainland, islanders now have access to efficient,

© Tourism Vancouver Island

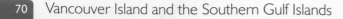

▲ Shawnigan Lake, a centre for water sports in summer. © *Pierre Longnus*

modern means of transportation. A number of ferries connect the islands and the mainland every day.

The history of Vancouver Island and the Southern Gulf Islands is an interesting amalgam of Aboriginal and European cultures. Contact began with the arrival of Captain Cook in Nootka Sound in 1778; other English and Spanish explorers followed, opening up a route to the rich territories of the Pacific Northwest, which would later become British Columbia and Alaska. Today, the place names evoke this meeting between Aboriginal (Cowichan, Sooke), English (Chatham, Cavendish) and Spanish (Galiano, Estevan) heritages.

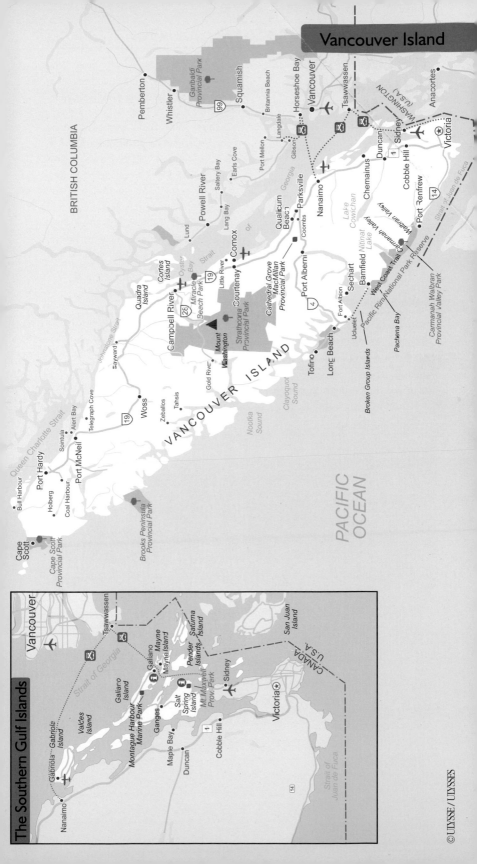

Vancouver Island

The Southern Gulf Islands

BRITISH COLUMBIA

VANCOUVER ISLAND

PACIFIC OCEAN

WASHINGTON (U.S.A.)

Strait of Georgia

Strait of Juan de Fuca

Queen Charlotte Strait

Johnstone Strait

Clayoquot Sound

Nootka Sound

Lake Cowichan

Nitinat Lake

Pemberton
Whistler
Squamish
Garibaldi Provincial Park
Britannia Beach
Horseshoe Bay
Vancouver
Tsawwassen
Anacortes
Langdale
Gibson
Port Mellon
Earls Cove
Saltery Bay
Sidney
Victoria
Duncan
Cobble Hill
Port Renfrew
Chemainus
Powell River
Lang Bay
Lund
Cathedral Grove
MacMillan Provincial Park
Qualicum Beach
Parksville
Nanaimo
Coombs
Port Alberni
Sechart
Bamfield
Fort Albion
West Coast Trail
Pacific Rim National Park Reserve
Pachena Bay
Carmanah Walbran Provincial Valley Park
Carmanah Valley
Walbran Valley
Comox
Little River
Courtenay
Strathcona Provincial Park
Miracle Beach Park
Campbell River
Cortes Island
Quadra Island
Oyster Bay
Sayward
Mount Washington
Gold River
Tofino
Long Beach
Ucluelet
Broken Group Islands
Woss
Zeballos
Tahsis
Telegraph Cove
Alert Bay
Sointula
Port McNeil
Coal Harbour
Holberg
Port Hardy
Bull Harbour
Cape Scott
Cape Scott Provincial Park
Brooks Peninsula Provincial Park

99
19
28
4
1
14

Vancouver
Tsawwassen
Gabriola Island
Valdes Island
Galiano Island
Galiano
Mayne
Mayne Island
Pender Island
Saturna Islands
Montague Harbour Marine Park
Ganges
Salt Spring Island
Mt. Maxwell Prov. Park
Maple Bay
Duncan
Cobble Hill
Sidney
San Juan Island
Victoria
Nanaimo
Gabriola
CANADA U.S.A.
1
14

© ULYSSE / ULYSSES

THE COWICHAN VALLEY ★ ★

Shawnigan Lake

This small town's main attribute is, of course, the lake of the same name. It is the largest body of water in the region. The other major attraction here is the **Kinsol Trestle ★ ★ ★**, one of the longest wooden railway bridges in the world. Built in 1921, it was once used for the transport of copper ore.

Lake Cowichan

Lake Cowichan is a small town built on the shores of the lake of the same name. Located 31km east of Duncan, it is easily reached via Highway 18. The lake was nicknamed *Kaatza* by the area's Aboriginals, which means "the big lake." Thirty kilometres long, it is one of the biggest lakes on the island.

Located some 50km west via a forest road, **Carmanah Walbran Park ★ ★ ★** is a magnificent wild expanse comprising close to 17,000ha of ancient forests. This protected area flourishes in the humid climate of the West Coast and boasts some of the world's tallest spruces, reaching almost 100m in height, as well as centuries-old Western red cedars.

FROM NANAIMO TO TOFINO ★ ★ ★

Nanaimo

Nanaimo is an important town because of its link to the continent, where ferries pick up hundreds of tourists head-

COWICHAN VALLEY WINES

Just south of the city of Duncan, on a wine route open to tourists, lie the vineyards whose wines are among the most renowned on Vancouver Island. Most properties are accessible from Highway 1, between Duncan and Victoria, and you can pay these wine growers a visit to sample their wares. The entrances are marked with specific road signs (often a bunch of grapes) that indicate where to make a turn.

The Cowichan Valley vineyards have slowly but surely acquired a good reputation. The region's mild climate, sandy beaches and peaceful bays, as well as the beauty of its rural landscapes, have attracted scores of poets and nature lovers. Wine growers from the world over increasingly covet this part of Vancouver Island, and many have managed to set themselves up here.

▲ MacMillan Provincial Park—Cathedral Grove and its enchanted forest. © *Pierre Longnus*

▶ Carmanah Walbran Provincial Park.
© *Pierre Longnus*

ed for this region. It lies 35km from Vancouver, across the Strait of Georgia, and 1h30min from Victoria by way of the Trans-Canada.

The **Harbourside Walkway** ★★, a pleasant promenade lined with parks, historic sites and shops, runs along the seaside in Nanaimo.

Coombs

When passing through Coombs, a stop at the **Butterfly World and Gardens** ★★ is an absolute must. The foremost artificial butterfly habitat in Canada, it features a man-made tropical forest that has been laid out in a controlled environment in order to allow 80 species of butterflies to flutter about in total freedom.

The route to Port Alberni passes through **MacMillan Provincial Park–Cathedral Grove** ★★, a wonderful, mystical place. The Douglas firs inhabiting this magnificent forest, some of which are over 800 years old, stand almost 80m tall. Cathedral Grove is considered a sacred place by Aboriginals.

Ucluelet ★

Located at the south end of Long Beach, Ucluelet is a tiny town whose main street is lined with old wooden houses. Over 200 species of birds can

From Nanaimo to Tofino

THE DOUGLAS FIR

The spectacular Douglas fir's scientific name is *Pseudotsuga menziesii*, referring to Archibald Menzies, the Scottish botanist and physician who discovered it in Western Canada in 1791.

Menzies first spotted this species in Nootka Sound, on what is now Vancouver Island, during Captain Vancouver's *Discovery* expedition to continue the exploration of the Pacific coast after the death of Captain James Cook. David Douglas, the Scottish botanist who gave the fir tree his name, rediscovered it in 1825 and introduced it to England and Europe. Today, the Douglas fir makes up close to 2.5% of the French forest, particularly in the Massif Central and Morvan, and is one of the main reforestation softwood species in Western Europe.

In North America, its land of origin, it covers a vast area from California to British Columbia, between the Pacific coast and the eastern face of the Rockies. The Douglas fir can live 500 years, and its straight trunk can grow to 80m high and several metres in diameter.

An excellent, durable wood for carpentry, Douglas fir is used in joinery work for floor boards, cabinets and more. It is also highly prized in ship-building for its size and the absence of knots and defects, and is also used in hydraulic and marine work (locks, piers, wharfs). And of course there are composite and plywood panels made of Douglas fir, which, along with poplar, is the most popular plywood in the construction industry.

◀ Douglas firs. © *Softwood Export Council*

▲ Pacific Rim National Park Reserve, Long Beach Unit. © *Pierre Longnus*

be found around Ucluelet. Migrating grey whales swim in the coves and near the beaches here between the months of March to May, making whale-watching one of the main attractions on the west coast.

At the south end of the village, in **He Tin Kis Park ★★**, there is a wooden walkway leading through a small temperate rain forest beside Terrace Beach. This short walk highlights the beauty of this type of vegetation.

Pacific Rim National Park Reserve, Long Beach Unit ★ ★ ★

Pacific Rim National Park Reserve, Long Beach Unit, generally simply referred to as Long Beach, begins just outside Ucluelet and follows the coast until just before Cox Bay, outside of Tofino. Along the way, it offers nine different trails, all less than 5km long and well indicated along the Pacific Rim Highway.

The park is trimmed with kilometres of deserted beaches running alongside temperate rain forests. The beaches,

hiking trails and various facilities are clearly indicated and easy to reach. The setting is enchanting, relaxing and stimulating at once, as well as being accessible year-round.

Bamfield ★

Situated on the Barkley Sound fjord on Vancouver Island's west coast, Bamfield is a charming, rather remote little village that can be reached from Port Alberni or Lake Cowichan via a network of forest roads that are dusty in summer and muddy in winter.

The region and its thousand-year-old forests are a little paradise for outdoor activity buffs and nature enthusiasts. Bamfield is also one of the starting points of the famous **West Coast Trail ★ ★ ★**, which cuts through Pacific Rim National Park. This trail extends over the southeast coast of Barkley Sound, between the villages of Bamfield and Port Renfrew. This "Lifesaving Trail," a 75km-long path, was laid out at the turn of the century to help rescue shipwrecked sailors whose vessels frequently crashed against the coast's ominous reefs.

Tofino ★

Tofino, situated at the northwest end of Long Beach, is a lively town where the many visitors chat about sunsets and the outdoors. Spanish explorers Galiano and Valdes, who discovered this coast in the summer of 1792, named the place after Vincente Tofino, their hydrography professor. From mid-March to mid-April, Tofino lives for the **Whale Festival**, a month in which the global grey whale population passes through the region. Every year, close to 19,000 grey whales undertake a 16,000km mi-

▲ Tofino opens onto the grandeur of the Pacific. © *Pierre Longnus*

gratory journey from the Baja California peninsula in Mexico, to the Bering and Chukchi Seas off Alaska and Siberia.

FROM TELEGRAPH COVE TO PORT HARDY ★ ★

Telegraph Cove ★ ★

This little slice of heaven, set back from the eastern shore of Vancouver Island, was once the end point of a telegraph line that ran along the coast. Later, a wealthy family set up a sawmill on land they had purchased around the little bay. From that point on, time seems

to have stopped; the little houses have been preserved, and the boardwalk alongside the bay is dotted with commemorative plaques explaining the major stages in the village's history.

▼ Telegraph Cove. © *Telegraph Cove Resorts*

THE GREY WHALE

The grey whale is one of the largest of its species: the female can reach up to 15m in length, and the male up to 14m. Their adult weight can range from 15 to 30 tons. The grey whale's diet consists mainly of shrimp and small fish, and it can

© iStockphoto.com / Dale Walsh

consume up to 1,200kg of food per day. In the spring of each year, thousands of visitors descend upon the Pacific Rim National Park Reserve in the Tofino area in the hopes of spotting grey whales off the shoreline as they travel north.

The grey whale's migration is the longest undertaken by a mammal: an impressive round trip of 19,500km between the northern waters of the Bering Sea and the warm waters of Mexico's Baja California peninsula, at a rate of 60km to 80km per day. From December to February, grey whales give birth to their young near Baja California. In mid-February, the females and the whale calves start their migration north, followed by the males. Certain whales start to feed upon reaching the waters that surround Vancouver Island; others wait for the approach of the Bering and Chukchi Seas off Alaska and Siberia. Over the summer spent in these glacial waters, grey whales create enormous reserves of food that can reach from 16% to 30% of their body weight. In October, the beginning of winter heralds the return migratory journey to Baja California, and the whales live from their stored provisions.

The grey whale virtually disappeared in the middle of the 1850s. Hunters abruptly abandoned the hunt, before taking it up again around 1914, once again virtually decimating the population. But since 1937, the grey whale has been a protected species.

Alert Bay ★ ★

At the **U'mista Cultural Center ★**, one can learn about the Potlatch ("to give") ceremony through the history of the U'mista Aboriginal community. Missionaries tried to ban the ceremony; there was even a law forbidding members of the community from dancing, preparing objects for distribution or making public speeches. The ceremony was then held in secret and during bad weather, when the missionaries couldn't get to the island. A lovely collection of masks and jewellery adorns the walls. The **Native Burial Grounds** and the **Memorial Totems ★ ★**, which testify to the richness of this art, should not be missed.

Port Hardy

Port Hardy, a town of fishers and forest workers, is located at the northeast end of Vancouver Island. There is a wealth of animal life in this region, both in the water and on the land. Visitors can go fishing or whale-watching here, or simply treat themselves to a walk through the forest in Cape Scott Provincial Park.

Cape Scott Provincial Park ★ ★ encompasses 15,070ha of temperate rain forest. Scott was a merchant from Bombay, India, who financed all sorts of commercial expeditions. Many ships have run aground on this coast, and a lighthouse was erected in 1960 in order to guide sailors safely along their way. Sandy beaches cover two-thirds of the 64km stretch of waterfront.

▼ The Southern Gulf Islands, with the Coast Mountains in the distance. © *Pierre Longnus*

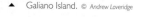

▲   Galiano Island. © *Andrew Loveridge*

THE SOUTHERN GULF ISLANDS ★ ★ ★

The Gulf Islands consist of some 200 islands scattered across the Strait of Georgia between the eastern shore of Vancouver Island and the west coast of the mainland. Among these are the Southern Gulf Islands, which have retained their wild essence and charm by not being overly commercially developed. With no concrete and few cars to mar their beauty, these islands constitute havens of peace for stressed-out Vancouverites and various bohemians.

Gabriola Island ★ ★

Nature dominates Gabriola Island, and the best way to appreciate its distinct atmosphere is to visit it by bike. This peaceful haven attracts many Nanaimo residents, several of whom have a home on the island, and its superb landscape provides a good spot for visitors to spend a few quiet days away from it all.

Salt Spring Island ★

With its many art galleries, restaurants and boutiques, Salt Spring Island is the most developed of the Gulf Islands. Aboriginals used to come here during summer to catch shellfish, hunt fowl and gather plants. In 1859, the first Europeans settled on the island and began establishing farms and small businesses here. During the summer, artists and artisans flood the streets, exhibiting their work. The Saturday market held in the small town of **Ganges** is also very popular.

Galiano Island ★ ★

The first thing one notices upon arriving on Galiano Island is the scarcity of infrastructure and commercial development. The inhabitants' passionate protests to protect the ecological balance of their island have attracted worldwide attention. Their efforts have enabled Galiano Island to preserve its vast stretches of untouched wilderness, which attract many bird lovers come springtime. The island is also home to several meditation centres and retreats for New Age enthusiasts.

The Southern Gulf Islands

Southern British Columbia

British Columbia's southern region, which borders on the United States, is characterized by a blend of the urban and the undeveloped. The Vancouver area, for example, resembles a big American city, though it is set against a backdrop of green mountains and blue sea; here, visitors will find both wilderness and civilization. For its part, the Okanagan Valley is home to countless orchards and some of the best wineries in the county.

As one majestic landscape succeeds another, visitors are dazzled by the sea, the everlasting snows and the spring colours, which appear very early in this region. Communing with nature is a memorable part of any trip in southern British Columbia. The waters that wash the deserted beaches beckon you to relax and let your mind wander. Stately trees stand guard over tranquil areas untouched by the forestry industry. Dotted with national and provincial parks stretched across the loveliest parts of the province, this region has an extremely varied landscape, with

© Cedar Creek Estate Winery / Brian Sprout

▲   A peaceful harbour on the Sunshine Coast. © *Tourism Powell River*

everything from perpetual snows to desert valleys to rivers teeming with fish. A trip to southern British Columbia offers a chance to explore towns and parks set between the sea and the sky and meet people from a wide range of cultures.

A large part of the existing territory of the province was once called "New Caledonia." The name was eventually rejected in favour of "British Columbia" however, because a French colony called New Caledonia already existed in the South Pacific. "Columbia" (from the Columbia River, which was named by American captain Robert Gray in honour of his ship *Columbia*) was then used as an unofficial designation of the southern portion of the British colony. The name "British Columbia" was decided upon by Queen Victoria and officially adopted in 1858.

Southern British Columbia

THE SUNSHINE COAST ★★

The Sunshine Coast runs along the Strait of Georgia, bounded by Desolation Sound to the north, the Coast Mountains to the east and Howe Sound farther south. Most people get to the Sunshine Coast by boat, as there are no roads linking Vancouver to these resort towns; the daily comings and goings are dictated by the ferry schedule. As a result, the mentality here is completely different.

Lund ★★

Lund is located at the beginning (or the end, depending on what direction you're heading in) of Highway 101; the other end, located some 15,000km to the south, is Puerto Montt, Chile! The town's port is magnificent, with its old hotel, adjoining shops and wooden promenade which skirts round the bay. Imagine a typical fishing village and your harbour will undoubtedly be filled with the fishing boats that are moored here. There are many activities to choose from here, from fishing and whale-watching trips to snorkelling.

◀   Savary Island. © *Tourism Powell River*

▼   Between the mountains and the sea...
    © *Tourism Powell River*

Lund also marks the entrance to the marvellous **Desolation Sound Marine Park ★★**, whose warm waters are perfect for observing a wide variety of marine animal species. More and more people also come here to go sea kayaking, an activity that even beginners can enjoy.

Savary Island ★★

Savary Island is one of the Northern Gulf Islands. It is accessible by water-taxi from Powell River. The distance of the crossing is about 20km. It is nicknamed British Columbia's Hawaii and Pleasure Island for its **white sand beaches ★★★** and crystal-clear waters that make swimming a pleasure. Large numbers of eagles visit the island, and seal colonies frequent its shores. Activities practised on Savary Island include walking, cycling, swimming and sunbathing, making it truly the perfect summer destination. Visitors here should forget their car and hop on a bike to explore this small island and discover its strong community spirit.

Skookumchuck Rapids ★★★

The Skookumchuck Rapids of Skookumchuck Narrows Provincial Park are definitely one of the Sunshine Coast's most spectacular features. When the tides change, the sea water rushes into the Skookumchuck Narrows Canyon as if it were a great funnel. Skookumchuck is a Chinook word that means "powerful water," the significance of which is clear when you see the rapids with your own eyes. These rapids are among the world's largest, and visitors sometimes get to watch kayakers literally surf on the waves.

The Sunshine Coast

THE COAST MOUNTAIN LOOP ★ ★

Magnificent panoramic views abound all along the coast. Whether you are travelling by car, train or ferry, a succession of fjords, mountains, forests and scenic viewpoints await. The Sea to Sky Highway (Highway 99) is a winding road used by many visitors who come to Whistler for sporting vacations in both winter and summer.

Brackendale ★

Only 70km north of Vancouver by the Sea to Sky Highway, Brackendale is actually a suburb of Squamish. It is recognized as the most significant **gathering**

▲   British Columbia's Coast Mountains.
© *Pierre Longnus*

▲   A bald eagle. © *Pierre Longnus*

▲　Garibaldi Provincial Park. © *Pierre Longnus*

site for bald eagles ★★★ in the world, ahead of the Chilkat Bald Eagle Reserve in Alaska.

Garibaldi Provincial Park ★★

Vast Garibaldi Provincial Park, which covers 195,000ha, is extremely popular with hikers. Among its more than 90km of trails are the beautiful Garibaldi Lake and Singing Pass trails. Highway 99 runs along the west side of the park, offering access to the various trails.

▲　The world-famous Whistler region.
© *Pierre Longnus*

Whistler ★★

Whistler attracts skiers, golfers, hikers, mountain bikers, windsurfers, paragliders and snowboarders from all over the world.

An impressive hotel complex graces the little village at the foot of Blackcomb and Whistler Mountains. Other amen-

ities at this internationally renowned resort include restaurants, shops, sports facilities and a convention centre. Whistler is popular in summer and winter alike, and each season offers its own assortment of activities. It has long been rated among the top North American winter sports resorts.

The Coast Mountain Loop

▲ Magnificent Seton Lake. © *Pierre Longnus*

The Coast Mountain Loop

Lillooet

During the Gold Rush, Lillooet was the most important place in British Columbia, considered Mile 0 of the Gold Rush Trail to Caribou Country. Miners and tradespeople came to this wild territory and took this dangerous route in the hopes of making a fortune.

Now Lillooet is a peaceful community of 2,800 inhabitants and is mostly known for its spectacular landscape.

In summer, visitors come here to fish and camp. They are attracted by the area's dry, warm climate, which provides a respite from the rainy weather that often dominates the neighbouring regions.

Located in the town museum beside the totem poles, the tourist office can provide information on the best fishing spots and how to get to magnificent **Seton Lake ★ ★ ★**.

Manning Provincial Park ★ ★

Manning Provincial Park is located on the boundary of the southwestern part of the province and the huge Thompson-Okanagan region. It lies 225km from Vancouver, making it a popular getaway for city dwellers in search of vast green spaces. The park is home to a resort as well as shelters, cottages and campsites.

FROM THE THOMPSON RIVER TO ROGERS PASS ★

Ashcroft

Ashcroft lies a few kilometres east of Highway 1, the starting point for gold prospectors heading north during the 1860s gold rush. Heading east after Ashcroft, the Trans-Canada makes its way to Kamloops, passing through Cache Creek and skirting Kamloops Lake on the way, and providing a view of the area's ginseng fields.

Located southeast of Ashcroft, **Highland Valley Copper** ★ ★ is one of the largest open-cut copper mines in the world. The industrial machinery and the equipment used to transport the ore are gigantic. Though the mine is not open to visitors, its lunar landscape can be clearly seen from the highway.

Revelstoke ★ ★

The history of Revelstoke is closely linked to the construction of the transcontinental railway, when many Italians

◄   The mountain town of Revelstoke.
     © Pierre Longnus

From the Thompson River to Rogers Pass

came here to apply their expertise in building tunnels. To this day, the town's residents rely mainly on the railroad for their income. Tourism and the production of electricity also play important roles in the economy of this magnificent town.

Mount Revelstoke National Park ★ ★

Mount Revelstoke National Park is teeming with trails that run through the forest. The level of difficulty varies; some trails run past centuries-old trees or lead to the tops of mountains, affording splendid panoramic views.

Glacier National Park ★ ★

Glaciers and snow dominate the landscape in Glacier National Park, where avalanches are common in winter. A few kilometres past the park's western extrance is the **Hemlock Grove Boardwalk ★ ★ ★**, a 600m-long wooden walkway that crosses a stand of western hemlock trees.

▲   Mount Revelstoke National Park in the heart of the Rockies. © *Parks Canada / Lynch, W.*

◀   Glacier National Park. © *Parks Canada / Lynch, W.*

▼   Rogers Pass and the Selkirk Mountains. © *Parks Canada / M. Matsushita*

Rogers Pass ★ ★

Rogers Pass was named after the engineer who discovered it in 1881. This mountain pass was originally supposed to serve as a passage between the east and the west, but after a number of catastrophes, during which avalanches claimed the lives of hundreds of people, the Canadian Pacific Railway company decided to build a tunnel instead. Over some 15km, visitors now travel through five long avalanche protection tunnels to get to the **Rogers Pass Discovery Centre ★**, where they can learn about the epic history of the railway.

OKANAGAN VALLEY ★ ★ ★

All sorts of natural treasures await discovery in this part of British Columbia. With its stretches of water and blanket of fruit trees, the Okanagan Valley, which runs north-south, is one of the most beautiful areas in the province. Okanagan wines have won a number of prizes, the orchards feed a good portion of the country, and the lakes and mountains are a dream come true for sports enthusiasts.

The climate is conducive to a wide variety of activities: the winters, mild in the cities and snowy in the mountains, can be enjoyed by all. In the spring, the fruit trees are in bloom, while in summer and fall, a day of fruit-picking is often followed by a dip in one of the many lakes.

Cathedral Provincial Park ★ ★

Cathedral Provincial Park (33,000ha) is located 30km southwest of Keremeos, in the southern part of the province

▲ One of the Okanagan Valley's orchards.
© Pierre Longnus

▲ Osoyoos Lake after the rain. © Pierre Longnus

right alongside the U.S. border. There are two distinct kinds of vegetation here—the temperate forest and the plant growth characteristic of the arid Okanagan region. At low altitudes, Douglas firs dominate the landscape, giving way to spruce and heather higher up. Deer, mountain goats and wild sheep sometimes venture out near the turquoise-coloured lakes.

Okanagan Valley

▲ Carefully chosen grapes for a quality wine.
© *Pierre Longnus*

◀ A vineyard worthy of a French château.
© *Pierre Longnus*

Osoyoos

Osoyoos lies at the bottom of the valley, flanked on one side by Osoyoos Lake and on the other by verdant slopes decked with orchards. It is located next to the U.S. border, in an arid climate more reminiscent of a Southwestern desert, or even southern Italy, than a Canadian town. The main attraction here is the exceptionally warm lake, where one can enjoy a variety of water sports during summer.

A tiny **desert** ★ ★ ★, made up of sage and antelope brush grasslands, pokes its toe into the Southern Okanagan Valley. It is an amazing sight in this part of Canada, and is the only one in the country. The unique wildlife and vegetation here bear witness to nature's endless store of surprises. Without irrigation, this valley would still be a desert and the orchards and vineyards would not have been able to thrive and bear fruit each year. The mini-desert is part of the same desert that begins in the Mexican states of Baja California and Chihuahua before crossing the western United States.

The Wine Route ★ ★ ★

The Thompson-Okanagan region offers a memorable opportunity to discover a completely original wine route. The landscape in particular is unique; the parched hills and valleys aren't the colour and shape that you would expect when touring vineyards. Vines flourish in this climate and everything possible has been done to make the most of the region, with fruitful results.

Two types of wine-producing distinguish the region. The most recent, which is being developed in the Similkameen Valley, is associated with farm cultivation and expansion of the fertile soil. The other, more traditional type in the large Okanagan Valley, is related to a proud heritage of wine growing dating to the 1800s.

This valley has similar characteristics to renowned German wine-producing areas. The presence of four lakes (Skaha, Osoyoos, Vaseux and Okanagan) creates a climate that is perfectly suited to producing quality wines. The clearly indicated wine route offers pleasant trips, among farms and orchards along Highway 97, revealing breathtaking views of Okanagan Lake at every turn.

This mouth-watering trail of discovery runs from Osoyoos to Salmon Arm, as each vineyard vies to offer the best reception and most elegant presentation.

Wines are available to sample. Medals, international awards and anything attesting to a wine's quality cover the walls of shops. Even if it costs a few dollars to try a few drops of ultra sweet ice wine, a local specialty made from grapes that are picked frozen at the beginning of winter, curious wine-lovers are happy to oblige.

▼　Kettle Valley Steam Railway.
© Don Weixl / Penticton & Wine Country

SOME VINEYARDS TO VISIT

Most of the region's vineyards are open to the public and offer free or paying wine tastings, especially during the tourist season. The following vineyards, large, small, or unique, are a sample of the treasures of this famous valley.

Kelowna

Calona Vineyards, easily accessible from downtown Kelowna, was the valley's very first commercial vineyard.

Quails' Gate Estate Winery is a family vineyard whose chardonnays and pinot noirs are particularly well regarded. The **Old Vines Restaurant** is one of the region's best restaurants.

Naramata

Elephant Island Orchard Wines produces wine not from grapes but from other fruits. Among their most popular varieties are the cherry wine and Fuji apple ice wine, which won't fail to impress you.

Lake Breeze Vineyards produces only about 6,000 cases of wine per year; their white wine is becoming more and more prominent. **The Patio** restaurant is worth a visit.

Laughing Stock Vineyards produces, among others, the excellent Portfolio, a blend of merlot and cabernet sauvignon, aged 20 months in oak casks.

Poplar Grove Wine & Cheese produces excellent wines and the perfect home-made cheeses to accompany them.

Olivier

Domaine Combret is run by a French wine family that has produced wine for generations. Their wines have received numerous awards.

Inniskillin Okanagan Vineyards, which also has a vineyard in Ontario, is reputed for its ice wine.

Osoyoos

NK'MIP Cellars is owned and managed by an aboriginal nation. Not only do they produce a well-regarded wine, but the view from the restaurant terrace is fantastic.

Peachland

Hainle Vineyards is an organic vineyard combined with a very active school of cuisine and a gastronomic restaurant.

Penticton

Red Rooster Winery, whose wines were served to Queen Elizabeth II when she visited the region in 2005, also hosts an art gallery.

Summerland

Sumac Ridge Estate Winery is one of the biggest vineyards of the region.

Westbank

Mission Hill Family Estate, a grand vineyard, is not to be missed.

▼ Bountiful grapes. © *Pierre Longnus*

The list of wineries is long and interesting. Over a short distance of 200km, there are more than 50 establishments, with new ones opening constantly. Some are active throughout the year, but a few are open to visitors only during the tourist season.

Penticton ★

Located between Okanagan Lake, to the north, and Skaha Lake, to the south Penticton boasts a dry, temperate climate. The area's First Nations named the site *Pen-tak-tin*, meaning "the place where you stay forever." People come to Penticton for the outdoor activities, fine dining and local *joie de vivre*. A beach lined with trees and a pedestrian walkway run along the north end of town, and the dry landscape, outlined by the curves of the sandy shoreline, contrasts with the surrounding vineyards and orchards.

An outing in the mountains along the former route of the **Kettle Valley Steam Railway ★ ★** offers another perspective of the Okanagan Valley. Laid at the turn of the 20th century, these tracks connected Nelson in the east to Hope in the west, thus providing a link between the coast and the hinterland, where tonnes of ore were being extracted.

Kelowna ★

Kelowna, the largest city in inland British Columbia, has a population of more than 111,000. Its economy is driven by forestry, fruit farming, wine making, manufacturing and, recently, a number of high-tech industries as well. Tourism is also important to Kelowna, and the town has a lot to offer its many visitors.

▲   A white-tailed deer. © *Pierre Longnus*

Kelowna is the heart of the Okanagan Valley. It was here that a French Oblate by the name of Father Charles Pandosy set up the first Catholic mission in the hinterland of British Columbia in 1859. He introduced apple and grape growing into the Okanagan Valley and was thus largely responsible for its becoming a major fruit-producing region.

The beautiful **sandy beaches** that border Okanagan Lake draw more and more visitors every year. They come here to lounge under a beautiful summer sky, organize a family picnic, or simply admire the scenery.

KOOTENAY ROCKIES ★ ★

Visit the Kootenay Rockies region and discover the spectacular landscapes of the Monashee, Selkirk and Purcell

Kootenay Rockies

▲ The Kootenay Rockies, a vast natural area of green and blue. © *Parks Canada / Lynch, W.*

Kootenay Rockies

mountains, with their meandering lakes and rivers. The area's winding roads often end abruptly on the shore of a lake, where visitors can board a ferry to the other side. This is part of the charm of the Kootenays, and may explain the slower pace than that found in the two large neighbouring tourism areas, the Rockies and the Okanagan Valley.

In the midst of nature at its purest, visitors can enjoy a variety of outdoor activities year-round in the Kootenays. Culture and history are not to be out-done though: the incredible silver era and other significant periods have left numerous traces here.

Sandon ★

At the turn of the century, 5,000 people lived and worked in Sandon. By 1930, the price of silver had dropped and the mine had been exhausted, prompting an exodus from the town. During World War II, Sandon became an internment centre for Japanese who had been living on the coast. Shortly after the war, it became a ghost town once again, and a number of buildings were destroyed by fire and floods. Today, visitors can admire what remains of a number of old buildings, as well as the first hydroelectric power plant constructed in the Canadian West, the **Silversmith Powerhouse**, which still produces electricity.

Kokanee Glacier Provincial Park ★ ★

Kokanee Glacier Provincial Park has some 85km of hiking trails of medium difficulty. The park is accessible from a number of different places.

Nelson ★ ★

Located at the southern end of the West Arm of Kootenay Lake, Nelson lies on the west flank of the Selkirk Mountains. In 1867, during the silver boom, miners set up camp here, working together to build hotels, homes and public facilities. Numerous buildings now bear witness to the town's prosperous past. Nelson has managed to continue its economic growth, thanks to light industry, tourism and the civil service.

The Visitor Info Centre distributes two small pamphlets that guide visitors through over 350 historic buildings. The town's elegant architecture makes walking here a real pleasure. Classical, Queen Anne and Victorian buildings proudly line the streets and provide eloquent reminders of the opulence of the silver mining era. Among the city's must-sees are the stained-glass windows of the **Nelson Congregational Church ★**, the group of buildings on **Baker Street**, the Italian-style **Fire Station ★** which dominates the city and the Chateau-style building that once housed the city hall and the post office and is now home to the **Touchstones Nelson**

▲ Kokanee Glacier Provincial Park.
© Kootenay Rockies Tourism

Museum of Art and History ★. The museum has displays on the local First Nations, explorers, miners, traders and settlers who shaped the city's history, as well as contemporary art exhibits.

Kootenay Rockies

▲ Fort Steele Heritage Town, in the heart of the mountains. © *Fort Steele Heritage Town / Bob Holm*

Creston Valley Wildlife Area ★ ★

The Creston Valley Wildlife Area is certainly worth stopping at. The internationally acclaimed conservation area is a 7,000ha fertile wetland, with yellow-headed blackbirds, western painted turtles and spotted frogs. More than 265 species of nesting and migratory birds can be viewed here, and an excellent one-hour guided canoe tour of the marshes is also offered.

Cranbrook

Conveniently located between the Okanagan Valley and Calgary, Cranbrook is situated on the plains between the Purcell and Rocky Mountains. The discovery of gold and the subsequent arrival of the Canadian Pacific Railway in 1898 made the community the region's main trading area, and it remains the main service centre for the East Kootenays.

Fort Steele Heritage Town ★ ★ is a wonderful reconstructed boomtown with 58 buildings, about 10km north of Cranbrook. The original community emerged with the gold rush; strife with the local Kootenay First Nation led the North-West Mounted Police to send Inspector Sam Steele, who built the barracks that became known as Fort Steele. The decision to take the railroad through Cranbrook instead of Fort Steele in 1898 sealed the town's fate, and by the end of World War II the population had dwindled to just 50.

Kootenay Rockies

Northern British Columbia

British Columbia has long been renowned for its exceptional and varied range of outdoor activities. Those who have a taste for adventure and exploring, or simply love nature, will be repeatedly delighted and surprised by the unspoiled, little-known northern part of the province.

Eighty percent of this territory is studded with mountains, many of which are perpetually covered with snow or glaciers. The lakes, which collect the run-off from the glaciers, are almost iridescent, while the forests are among the most renowned in the world. These enchanting surroundings offer seemingly endless possibilities for outdoor activities.

Only three major roads lead through these vast northern spaces. The Stewart-Cassiar Highway (Highway 37), to the west, passes through the heart of the North by Northwest region. The Alaska Highway, in

the east, starts at Dawson Creek. Finally, the Yellowhead Highway (Highway 16) runs along the southern part of these two regions, all the way to the shores of the Pacific, where visitors can set out for the Queen Charlotte Islands.

The starting point of any visit to northern British Columbia is the city of Prince George. From there north, the summer days grow noticeably longer. This phenomenon becomes more and more evident the farther north you go. The summertime sky never darkens completely, and depending on where you find yourself, you might even see the midnight sun.

THE CARIBOO MOUNTAINS AND THE CHILCOTIN HIGHWAY ★ ★

The Cariboo Mountains' must-see attractions can be found east of Quesnel on Highway 26, while the Chilcotin Highway leads to spectacular Tweedsmuir Provincial Park and the Bella Coola Valley, home to the only seaport between Prince Rupert and Vancouver Island.

Williams Lake

Nicknamed *The Hub of the Cariboo*, Williams Lake is smack in the centre of this vast region. The city, which now lives mainly from forestry, developed thanks to the construction of the Pacific Great Eastern Railway's railroad in 1919. This period also saw the first **Williams Lake Stampede** in 1920. Almost as popular as the famous Calgary Stampede, this rodeo attracts the top American cowboys and plenty of spectators each year, doubling the city's population while it's on.

◀ The majestic caribou.
© Pierre Longnus

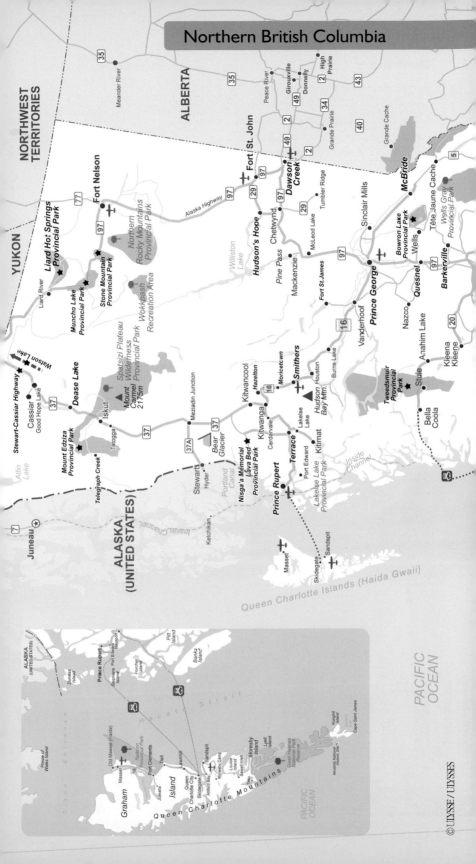

Northern British Columbia

Quesnel ★ ★ ★

Located 120km north of Williams Lake, Quesnel's tree- and flower-lined streets and its location at the confluence of the Quesnel and Fraser rivers make it the most beautiful town in the region.

Like many other towns in the area, Quesnel experienced the 19th-century Gold Rush. Gold diggers stocked up on foodstuffs and survival gear in Quesnel before heading off to look for those famous nuggets in the distant valleys, which is how Quesnel got its nickname "Gold Pan City." Today, the forest indus-try has replaced the mining industry as the economic engine for the region. More than 2,000 families rely on it for their livelihood.

A stunning attraction awaits at **Pinnacles Provincial Park**. A 20min walk through the evergreen forest leads to a group of sandy pillars called "hoodoos." These unusual earth-toned vertical formations date back some 12 million years, when they were formed by the erosion of several layers of volcanic ash. Today, only the strongest layers remain intact as they proudly thrust up into the sky.

Barkerville ★ ★ ★

Barkerville sprung up out of nowhere in 1862 when Billy Barker discovered gold in William's Creek. During the eight years that followed, 100,000 people came here to try their luck, making Barkerville the largest town west of Chicago and north of San Francisco.

◀   Welcome to Quesnel! © *April Cheng*

▼   The preserved frontier town of Barkerville.
   © *BC Heritage*

▲   En route to the unknown.... © *Pierre Longnus*

DRIVING IN NORTHERN BRITISH COLUMBIA

Most of the northern highways in British Columbia are paved. Some portions of the Stewart-Cassiar Highway and the Alaska Highway, however, are gravel. Flat tires are common so it is important to check your spare tire.

Bring along an antiflat spray as tire repair workshops are relatively uncommon. Ensure that your vehicle is in good working order before heading out. A tow to the nearest town and waiting around for parts from Vancouver will cost you a lot of time and money.

Fill up your gas tank whenever you can since gas stations are rare. Take a 25-litre jerry can just to be sure. Don't forget to buckle up and keep your headlights on at all times for better visibility on the sometimes dusty long straight stretches.

Unfortunately, the reserves were eventually exhausted. Today, the town is a protected historic site named **Barkerville Historic Town**, where more than 125 buildings have been restored to their original frontier-town look. The result is striking: saloon, hotel, post office, printer and blacksmith. Everything here is a perfect illusion. Or is it? Still today, gold prospectors can be found panning the bottom of the river that flows through the region.

At Barkerville, a network of trails follows the paths taken by the original gold diggers. The wilderness is still relatively untouched and the flora and fauna are breathtaking. The prospectors' old cabins can be found along the path.

Bowron Lake Provincial Park ★ ★ ★

Located 27km east of Barkerville, magnificent Bowron Lake Provincial Park covers some 122,000ha and is particularly popular with canoers and kayakers for its lakes and waterways. Also a wildlife sanctuary, the park is a good spot to observe moose, deer and mountain goats.

Tweedsmuir Provincial Park ★ ★ ★

Tweedsmuir Provincial Park lies 360km northwest of Williams Lake on Highway 20. One of the largest parks in British Columbia, it is an untouched paradise blanketed with lakes, greenery and mountains. Visitors can cross this slice of heaven along a network of trails, with hikes that can last from several hours to a month. One of the park's most breathtaking sights is without a doubt the view of **Hunlen Falls ★ ★ ★**, which is accessible along a 16.4km trail.

The Bella Coola Valley ★ ★

Beyond Tweedsmuir Provincial Park, the Chilcotin Highway reaches the Bella Coola Valley. This is where explorer Alexander Mackenzie completed his crossing of Canada in 1793. To mark his journey, he created one of Western Canada's most famous pieces of graffiti: *Alexander Mackenzie, from Canada, by land, 22 July 1793*. Initially a Hudson's Bay Company trading post, the town of **Bella Coola** became a major fishing port under the influence of its first Norwegian inhabitants.

FROM PRINCE GEORGE TO DAWSON CREEK

Beginning from Prince George, Highway 97 leads to Dawson Creek, kilometre 0 (what some people call "mile 0") of the Alaska Highway. The region developed largely around forestry and hydroelectricity. The highway runs through lovely lake-strewn woods and crosses the Rocky Mountains. It's not uncommon to encounter bears and moose here, particularly when travelling through provincial parks.

Prince George ★ ★

With its population of 77,000, Prince George considers itself the capital of northern British Columbia. As any map will tell you, however, it actually lies in the centre of the province. Its geographic location has made it a hub not only for the railway, but also for road transport, since it lies at the crossroads of Highway 16, which runs the width of the province, and Highway 97, which runs the length.

▲   A mountain landscape on Highway 97.
    © Pierre Longnus

▸   The Grand Trunk Bridge at Prince George.
    © Initiatives Prince George

The Exploration Place ★★ is located on the site where Fort George was built in 1807, in the park that bears the same name. The most important museum and science centre in northern British Columbia, it is the ideal place to learn more about the history of Prince George. With its many interactive exhibitions on regional wildlife, sports and palaeontology, the centre appeals to young and old, no matter what their interests.

Hudson's Hope ★★

This area was first explored in 1793 by Alexander Mackenzie. In 1805, a fur-trading post was set up here. Nowadays, Hudson's Hope is known mainly for its hydroelectric complexes, one of which was built in the 1960s (W.A.C. Bennett), the other slightly more recently (Peace Canyon).

Of course, the major points of interest in Hudson's Hope are the **W.A.C. Bennett** ★★ and **Peace Canyon** ★★ hydroelectric facilities. Free tours are available at both. A hodgepodge of stone and concrete that fills a natural valley, the W.A.C. Bennett dam is one of the world's largest structures, while its reservoir, Williston Lake, is the world's ninth largest artificial body of water!

From Prince George to Dawson Creek

▲   Dawson Creek. © *Pierre Longnus*

◄   The W. A. C. Bennett Dam and Williston Reservoir. © *BC Hydro*

Dawson Creek ★

Dawson Creek was named after Dr. George Dawson, a geologist who, in 1879, discovered that the surrounding plains were ideal for agriculture. He might have thought that Dawson Creek would become a farming capital, but he probably never suspected that oil and natural gas would be discovered here.

The other major turning point in Dawson Creek's history took place in 1942, when the town became kilometre/mile 0 of the Alaska Highway. Today, nearly 30,000 tourists from all over the world come to Dawson Creek every year to start their journey northward.

The **Dawson Creek Station Museum ★**, which traces the history of the Alaska Highway and of the area's first inhabitants, and the **Dawson Creek Art Gallery**, which displays handicrafts and works by local artists in an immense grain elevator, are both part of **Northern Alberta Railway Park (NAR) ★★**.

THE ALASKA HIGHWAY ★★★

Paved and well-maintained, the Alaska Highway offers visitors from all over the world an unhoped-for access to majestic landscapes. Before setting out, though, travellers should make sure that their car's engine and tires are in good condition, since there aren't very many repair

THE ALASKA HIGHWAY

The Alaska Highway started out as a war measure. The Americans, who initiated the project, wanted to create a communication route that would permit the transport of military equipment, provisions and troops by land to Alaska. Construction started in March 1942, in the village of Dawson Creek, which had only 600 inhabitants at the time. Within a few weeks, over 10,000 people, mostly military workers, had flooded into the area. Over 11,000 American soldiers and engineers, 16,000 civilian workers and 7,000 machines and tractors of every description were required to clear a passage through thousands of kilometres of wilderness. The cost of this gargantuan project, which stretched 2,436km and included 133 bridges, came to $140 million (CAD). Even today, the building of the Alaska Highway is viewed as a feat of engineering on a par with the Panamá Canal. The Canadian section (Highway 97) remained under military supervision until 1964.

Today, this extraordinary highway is a vital social and economic link for all northern towns. It also offers tourists from all over the world unhoped-for access to the majestic landscapes of this region.

▼   The endless forest landscape of the Alaska Highway. © *Pierre Longnus*

shops along the way. Furthermore, a lot of roadwork is carried out during summer, and the resulting dust can make driving conditions difficult. It is therefore better to leave your headlights on at all times.

Stone Mountain Provincial Park ★ ★ ★

The entrance to Stone Mountain Provincial Park is located at the highest point on the Alaska Highway, at an altitude of 1,267m. It covers 25,690ha of rocky peaks, geological formations and lakes, and is home to the largest variety of animal life in northern British Columbia.

Muncho Lake Provincial Park ★ ★ ★

Muncho Lake is one of the loveliest provincial parks in Canada and definitely one of the highlights on the British Columbian portion of the Alaska Highway. It encompasses 86,079ha of bare, jagged mountains around magnificent Muncho Lake, which stretches over 12km. Like all the parks in the region, it owes its existence to the Alaska Highway. Large numbers of beavers, black bears, grizzlies, wolves and mountain goats make their home here, while the magnificent plant life includes a variety of orchids. There are almost no trails in the park, so the best way to explore it is along the Alaska Highway.

Liard Hot Springs Provincial Park ★ ★ ★

Liard Hot Springs Provincial Park is the most popular place for travellers to stop along the Alaska Highway. Here, they can relax in natural pools fed by 52°C hot springs. The microclimate created by the high temperature of the water, which remains constant in summer and winter alike, has enabled a unique assortment of plants to thrive here. Giant ferns and a profusion of carnivorous plants give the area a slightly tropical look.

▼ The untamed wilderness of Stone Mountain Provincial Park. © *Pierre Longnus*

◄ Alaska Highway Signpost Forest.
© *Pat Reece / yukoninfo.com*

THE CHILKOOT TRAIL

The Yukon's most famous hike starts in Alaska and ends ... in British Columbia. The Chilkoot Trail is the route that most gold prospectors took to cross the mountains and reach the interior lakes that flow into the Yukon River. At the time, gold prospectors had to bring everything they needed to survive for a year, which meant some 800kg of equipment they needed to carry or have carried. Their goal was to arrive at Lake Bennett in northern British Columbia by fall to spend the winter there. In the spring they followed the lake and then the river to Dawson. Many died as a result of falling behind schedule, because of an accident or through simple bad luck.

▶ On the Chilkoot Trail.
© Parks Canada / Lynch, W.

Watson Lake (Yukon) ★ ★ ★

Around 1897, an Englishman by the name of Frank Watson set out from Edmonton to lead the adventurous life of a gold-digger in Dawson City. After passing through regions that hadn't even been mapped yet, he ended up on the banks of the Liard River. He decided to stop his travels there and take up residence on the shores of the lake that now bears his name.

A visit to the **Alaska Highway Interpretive Centre** ★ ★ is a must for anyone interested in the history of the Alaska Highway. The epic story of the famous highway comes to life through a slide show and photographs.

The **Alaska Highway Signpost Forest** ★ ★ ★ is far and away the main attraction in Watson Lake. It is a collection of over 50,000 signs from the world over, placed on the posts by the tourists themselves. Some of them are highly original. Travellers who are planning a trip to the region can create their own sign in advance, or have one made on the spot for a few dollars.

THE STEWART-CASSIAR HIGHWAY ★ ★ ★

Completed in 1972, the Stewart-Cassiar Highway (Highway 37) is the trucking route used to bring supplies to communities in the northern part of the province and beyond. While the trip is a bit shorter than the Alaska Highway, the scenery is equally magnificent.

The Road to Stewart ★ ★ ★

Heading out from Meziadin Junction along the Stewart-Cassiar Highway, travellers can reach Alaska (U.S.A.) by following Highway 37A, aptly nicknamed the Glacier Highway. You will notice a major change in the scenery along the way. The mountains, with their snow- and glacier-capped peaks, look more and more imposing the closer you get.

Exactly 23km from Meziadin Junction, around a bend in the road, you will be greeted by the spectacular sight of **Bear Glacier ★ ★ ★**, which rises in all its azure-coloured splendour out of the milky waters of Strohn Lake at the same level as the road!

Nineteen kilometres further lies **Stewart ★ ★ ★**, a frontier town located just 2km from the little village of Hyder, Alaska. Both communities lie at the end of the 145km-long **Portland Canal**, the fourth deepest fjord in the world. In addition to forming a natural border between Canada and the United States, this narrow stretch of water gives Stewart direct access to the sea, making this little town, surrounded on all sides by towering, glacier-studded mountains, the most northerly ice-free port in Canada. In summer, the mild temperature is governed by the occasion-

▲ Bear Glacier ensconced amid the rocks.
© *Pierre Longnus*

▶ Peaks covered with perpetual snow tower over the Portland Canal. © *Pierre Longnus*

ally damp Pacific climate, while heavy snowfall is common in the winter (over 20m total).

Mount Edziza Provincial Park ★ ★ ★

Heading back north from Meziadin Junction along the Stewart-Cassiar Highway, travellers will cross Mount Edziza Provincial Park. Covering 260,000ha in the northwest part of the province, west of the Iskut River and

south of the Stikine River, the park is most notable for its volcanic sites, the most spectacular in all of Canada.

Dease Lake

Dease Lake is the largest community on the Stewart-Cassiar Highway. It is known as the jade capital of the world, due to the large number of quarries that surround the village. Lovely handcrafted sculptures are available in the many shops along the highway. Dease Lake is also an important industrial centre and a hub for government services.

Above all, this is a place to enjoy outdoor activities. Vast **Dease Lake** ★★★, 47km long, is ideal for trout and pike fishing, as well as being the point of departure for plane and horseback rides in Mount Edziza Provincial Park and the Spatsizi Plateau Wilderness Park.

Telegraph Creek ★★★

It is worth going to Telegraph Creek, if only for the pleasure of driving there. Laid in 1922, the winding road leads through some splendid scenery. The village at the end beckons visitors back in time to the pioneer era.

THE YELLOWHEAD HIGHWAY ★★★

The Yellowhead is an impressive highway (Route 16) that starts in Winnipeg, Manitoba, runs through Saskatchewan and Alberta, and ends at Prince Rupert. This tour covers the section between McBride, in eastern British Columbia and Prince Rupert, in the westernmost part of the province.

The incredibly varied scenery along the way includes high mountains, canyons, valleys and dense forests, providing an excellent overview of the geology and topography of British Columbia.

McBride

This little working-class community is sustained by the forest industry. It lies in a pleasant setting at the foot of the Rockies, on the banks of the Fraser River. We recommend walking up to the overlook at **Teare Mountain** ★★★, which offers an unimpeded view of the region.

Fort St. James

Fort St. James lies about 60km from the Yellowhead Highway via Hwy. 27. Its main claim to fame is **Fort St. James National Historic Site** ★★, an authentic trading post established by the Hudson's Bay Company in 1896. Actors in period dress and restored buildings (fur warehouse, workers' house, fish cache) recreate the atmosphere of bygone days.

Smithers ★★

Smithers is a pretty, pleasant town with unique architecture. The mountain setting, dominated by glacier-capped Hudson Bay Mountain, is splendid. Since its reconstruction in 1979, the town has taken on the look of a Swiss village. For this reason, many Europeans, lured by the local atmosphere and way of life, are among the town's residents.

The city's Central Park Building is home to the **Bulkley Valley Museum** ★★, which exhibits objects used by the

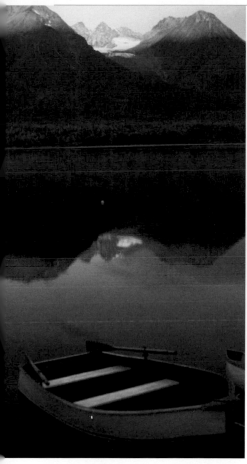

◀ The Stikine River at Telegraph Creek.
  © Andrew Webber

▲ The natural attractions around Smithers.
  © Pierre Longnus

▲ McBride. © Matthew G. Wheeler

pioneers and photographs from the local archives, as well as the **Smithers Art Gallery**.

Another interesting place to visit is **Driftwood Canyon Provincial Park ★★**, a major fossil site. In September, Smithers hosts the **Bulkley Valley Exhibition ★★★**, one of the largest agricultural fairs in British Columbia.

Moricetown Canyon and Falls ★★★

Along the Bulkley River, 40km west of Smithers on Aboriginal land, there is a fishing area known as Moricetown Canyon, which has been used by Aboriginals for centuries. Today, the Aboriginal people still use the same fishing methods as their ancestors. Using long poles with hooks on them, they catch onto the salmon, then trap them in nets as they swim upstream. This is a very popular place to take pictures.

Hazelton ★★

Hazelton is the largest of three neighbouring villages, the other two being South Hazelton and New Hazelton. Inhabited mainly by Aboriginal people, these three communities date back to the late 19th century, when the Hudson's Bay Company established a fur-trading post in the area (1868).

The Yellowhead Highway

▲ Anglers in Moricetown Canyon.
© Tourism Smithers

▲ An age-old salmon fishing technique.
© Tourism Smithers

▶ The Ksan Historical Village and Museum.
© Pierre Longnus

Today, the three villages are mainly known for the **Ksan Historical Village and Museum** ★★★, a reconstruction of a Gitksan village that shows the way of life and culture of this ancestral community. Here, visitors get a chance to admire their houses and totem poles, watch artists at work and even try traditional dishes.

Terrace ★★

Terrace is one of the larger towns on the Yellowhead Highway. It lies on the banks of the magnificent Skeena River, the second largest river in the province after the Fraser, and is surrounded by the Coast Mountains. Terrace is typical of a community dedicated to work, in that little effort has been put into making the town pretty and inviting. The surrounding scenery, on the other hand, is splendid.

An interesting attraction in Terrace is the **Heritage Park Museum** ★★, an open-air museum which deals with the history of the pioneers. There are a number of period buildings here, including a hotel, a barn, a theatre and six log cabins. Most date from 1910.

Nisga'a Memorial Lava Bed Provincial Park ★★★

Located some 100km north of Terrace on the Nisga'a Highway, the Nisga'a Memorial Lava Bed Provincial Park is the only natural site of its kind in Canada. Here, visitors will find a stunning 3km-wide and 10km-long lava

▲   A breathtaking landscape near Terrace. © *Andrew Webber*

field. Turquoise-coloured water resurgences on the surface add a bit of colour to this lunar landscape.

Lakelse Lake Provincial Park ★ ★

Located on Highway 37 halfway between Terrace and Kitimat, Lakelse Lake Provincial Park is the perfect spot for travellers looking to relax. A splendid sandy beach can be found on the shores of the magnificent lake for which the park is named.

From Terrace to Prince Rupert ★ ★ ★

The 132km stretch of highway between Terrace and Prince Rupert is undoubtedly one of the loveliest in Canada. The road follows the magnificent **Skeena River** almost curve for curve as it peacefully weaves its way between the **Coast Mountains**. On fine days, the scenery is extraordinary. Rest and picnic areas have been laid out all along the way.

Prince Rupert ★ ★ ★

The landscape changes radically near Prince Rupert. Huge hills covered with vegetation typical of the Pacific coast (large cedars, spruce trees) stretch as far as the eye can see. There is water everywhere, and although visitors will feel surrounded by lakes, what they actually see is the ocean creeping inland. A look at a map reveals that there are thousands of islands and fjords in this region. In fact, the town of Prince Rupert itself is located on an island, Kaien Island, 140km south of Ketchikan (Alaska). Prince Rupert is the most northerly point serviced by BC Ferries, and an important terminal for ferries from Alaska (Alaska Marine Highway).

The scenery is quite simply superb; mountains blanketed by dense forest encircle the town, and a splendid **natural harbour**, the second largest in the Canadian West, remind visitors that they have reached the coast. The history of Prince Rupert dates back to 1905, when engineers from the Grand Trunk Pacific Railway (GTPR), the transcontinental railroad, came here to look into the possibility of ending the line here.

Over 19,000km of possible routes were studied before it was decided that the railroad would in fact run alongside the Skeena River. Charles Hays, president of the GTPR, held a contest to christen the new terminus. The name Prince Rupert was chosen from nearly 12,000 entries, in honour of the explorer and first head of the Hudson's Bay Company, a cousin of Charles II of England.

Today, Prince Rupert is a lovely, prosperous community unlike any other town in northern British Columbia. Visitors won't find any concrete or garish neon signs here; instead, they are be greeted by opulent-looking Victorian architec-

▼   Prince Rupert. © *Pierre Longnus*

▼   The Skeena River and Coast Mountains.
    © *VIA Rail / Matthew G. Wheeler*

▲ The natural harbour of Prince Rupert.
© *Pierre Longnus*

▲ The Seal Cove seaplane landing at Prince Rupert. © *Lonnie Wishart Photography*

ture, large, pleasant streets, lovely shops and numerous restaurants reflecting a cosmopolitan atmosphere.

The interesting **Museum of Northern British Columbia** ★★ displays various artifacts, as well as magnificent works of art and jewellery, which serve as proof that Aboriginal people have been living in this region for over 5,000 years. The gift shop, located inside the museum, features a vast selection of books on indigenous art, as well as displaying crafts and paintings.

The picturesque neighbourhood of **Cow Bay** ★★★, built on piles and overlooking a pretty sailing harbour, is a must-see. All sorts of shops, cafes and restaurants are clustered together in a colourful seaside setting.

The **Seafest** takes place on the second weekend in June. Paraders march through the streets and sporting activities are held all weekend.

THE QUEEN CHARLOTTE ISLANDS (HAIDA GWAII) ★ ★ ★

The Queen Charlotte Islands archipelago consists of 150 islands of various sizes. Almost all of the urban areas are located on the largest one, **Graham Island**, to the north. **Moresby Island** is the second most populous. Here, visitors will find two villages, Sandspit and Alliford Bay, as well as the amazing Gwaii Haanas National Park Reserve.

The jagged relief of the Queen Charlotte and San Christoval Mountains has always protected the east coast from the westerly storms. Despite the weather, the Haida, who already inhabited the archipelago, established living areas on the west coast some 10,000 years ago. The Haida are known to this day for their high-quality handicrafts and beautiful works of art.

The Queen Charlotte Islands are also a great bird-watching destination, as they are home to the largest concentration of peregrine falcons in North America. Great herons and bald eagles, furthermore, are as common a sight around local villages as pigeons are in the big cities to the south.

Graham Island ★ ★ ★

Skidegate ★ ★ is the first place you'll see if you take the ferry to the Queen Charlotte Islands, since the landing stage is located at the edge of the village. Skidegate is a small Haida community of 470 inhabitants, located on the beach in the heart of **Roonay Bay**. While you're here, make sure to visit the internationally renowned **Haida Gwaii Museum** ★ ★ ★, devoted exclusively to articles made by the Haida over the ages, up until the present day.

▼ Bird's eye view of the Queen Charlotte Islands (Haida Gwaii). © *iStockphoto.com / Jason Verschoor*

▲ Hot Springs Island, a Haida heritage site. © *Parks Canada*

The Queen Charlotte Islands (Haida Gwaii)

All modes of expression are represented here: everything from totem poles, sculptures and drawings to fabrics and basketry, not to mention jewellery made with precious metals.

In the opposite direction, 1km north, is a local curiosity called **Balance Rock**, a bolder perched at the centre of an attractive pebble beach.

Located 4km south of Skidegate, **Queen Charlotte City** ★★ is a pleasant coastal village. The atmosphere is very relaxed here, and the streets are filled with young people during the summer season. The main attractions here are the ocean, the forest, the wildlife (eagles are everywhere) and exploring the coasts in the footsteps of the Haida Nation.

Moresby Island ★★

The **Gwaii Haanas National Park Reserve** ★★★ cannot be reached by land. This park, located at the southern tip of the archipelago, is home to many unusual sights, each more remarkable than the last. First, there is **Hot Springs Island**, a paradise for anyone who enjoys a good soak. Then there's **Laskeek Bay**, frequented by dolphins and whales. **Ninstints**, a former Haida village on the tip of the island of Sgan Gwaii, is a UNESCO World Heritage Site. It boasts the largest collection of totem poles and Aboriginal-built structures in the Queen Charlotte Islands, and there is something unreal and mystical about the location itself.

The Rocky Mountains

A chain of high mountains reaching elevations of between 3,000m and 4,000m and consisting of ancient crystalline rock that has been thrust upwards and then later carved out and eroded by glaciers, the Canadian Rockies run along the border between Alberta and British Columbia. Along with the Columbia Mountains and the Coast Mountains, which span almost all of British Columbia from north to south, the Rockies are Western Canada's largest mountain range.

Stretching over more than 170,000km^2, this vast region is known the world over for its natural beauty and welcomes millions of visitors each year. Exceptional mountain scenery, wild rivers perfect for white-water rafting, still lakes whose waters vary from emerald green to turquoise blue, parks abounding in all sorts of wildlife, world-renowned ski centres and quality resort hotels all come together to make for an unforgettable vacation.

"If we can't export the scenery, we'll import the tourists!" This statement by William

© Philippe Renault

Cornelius Van Horne, vice-president of the Canadian Pacific Railway, pretty well sums up the situation. The economy of the Canadian Rockies and Alberta's and British Columbia's national parks relies almost solely on tourism. The preservation of these areas is assured by their status as national parks, which also guarantees the complete absence of any type of industrial development, be it mining or forestry related. In fact, coal, copper, lead and silver mines as well as ochre deposits were abandoned and villages were moved in order to return the mountains to their original state and to stop human industry from destroying this natural beauty.

BANFF NATIONAL PARK AND BOW VALLEY PARKWAY ★ ★ ★

Banff National Park ★ ★ ★

The **Cave and Basin National Historic Site** ★ ★ ★ bears witness to the inextricable link that exists between the history of the Canadian Pacific Railway and that of the Rocky Mountains' national parks.

The cave, which still can be visited, was first discovered in November of 1883 by three Canadian Pacific workers after they abandoned a railway construction site to head off in search of gold. When brothers William and Tom McCardell and Frank McCabe reached Sulphur Mountain, however, they discovered sulphur hot springs instead. They took a concession in order to turn a profit with the springs, but were unable to counter the various land rights disputes that followed. The series of events drew the attention of the federal government, which sent out an agent to control the concession.

The renown of these hot springs had already spread from railway workers to the vice-president of Canadian Pacific, who came here in 1885 and declared that the springs were certainly worth a million dollars. Realizing the enormous economic potential of the hot springs, the federal government quickly purchased the rights to the concession from

◀   Bighorn sheep. © iStockphoto.com / Joseph Gareri

The Rockies

32

22

16

16

Edmonton

Hinton

Robb

Pocahontas

ALBERTA

Miette Hot Springs

Jasper National Park

Cadomin

16 Jasper

Medicine Lake

93

Rocky Mountain Forest Reserve

Sunwapta Falls

Maligne Lake

Bighorn Wildland Recreation Area

5

11

Athabasca Glacier

Icefields Parkway

White Goat Wilderness Area

Mica Creek

Mount Columbia 3747m

Columbia Icefield

Bighorn Wildland Recreation Area

Saskatchewan River Crossing

Siffleur Wilderness Area

Banff National Park

BRITISH COLUMBIA

1

Yoho National Park

Lake Louise

Bow Valley Parkway

Johnston Canyon

23

Glacier National Park

Golden

Field

1a

Mount Revelstoke National Park

Moraine Lake

Castle Mountain

Vermilion Pass

Banff

95

Canmore

Revelstoke

Marble Canyon

Calgary

1

Mount Assiniboine Provincial Park

Kananaskis Valley

23

Kootenay National Park

Beaton

Galena Bay

93

Shelter Bay

Radium Hot Springs

95

©ULYSSE / ULYSSES

the three workers and consolidated its property rights on the site by creating a nature reserve the same year.

Two years later, in 1887, the nature reserve became Canada's first national park. First named Rockies Park, it was subsequently rechristened Banff National Park. Today, it is the most well-known and visited of Canadian parks. Though incredibly beautiful, its renown also means it is generally overrun with visitors from all over the world.

Banff ★ ★ ★

At first glance, Banff looks like a small town made up essentially of hotels, motels, souvenir shops and restaurants all lined up along Banff Avenue. The town has much more to offer, however.

To accommodate the many rich tourists who flocked to Cave and Basin's hot springs at the end of the 19th century, tourist infrastructures and luxury hotels were built. The most prestigious of these was the **Banff Springs Hotel ★ ★ ★**, now known as the Fairmont Banff Springs, which certainly deserves a visit.

The **Cascade Gardens ★ ★** offer a marvellous view of Mount Cascade. The gardens' spectacular landscape includes arbours, waterfalls and a lovely selection of colourful annual and perennial flowers.

The **Buffalo Nations Luxton Museum ★ ★** is dedicated to the lives of the Aboriginal peoples of the northern plains and the Canadian Rockies.

WHY ARE THE CAVE AND BASIN SPRINGS HOT?

By penetrating into fissures in the rock, water makes its way under the western slope of Sulphur Mountain, absorbing calcium, sulphur and other minerals along the way. At a certain depth, the heat of the earth's centre warms the water as it is being forced up by pressure through a fault in the northeastern slope of the mountain. As the water flows up to the surface, the calcium settles around the source in pale-coloured layers that eventually harden into rock, called "tufa." These formations can be seen on the mountainside, at the small exterior spring located near the entrance to **Cave and Basin National Historic Site**.

◄ Cave and Basin National Historic Site and its open-air mineral water pool. © Travel Alberta

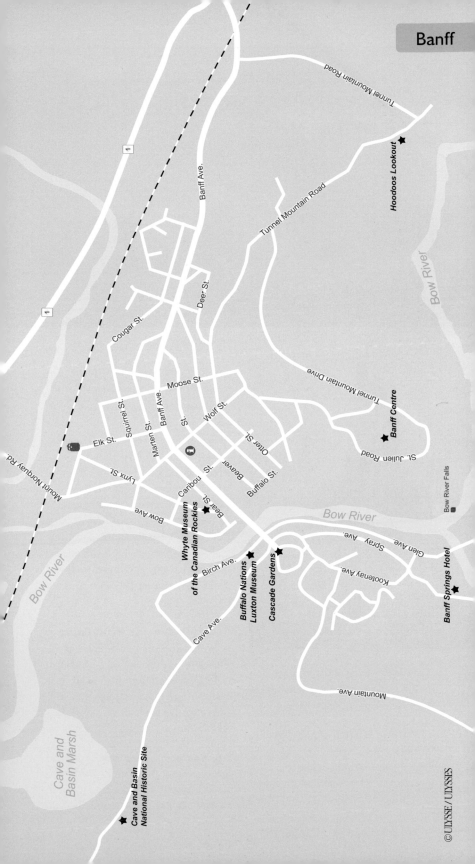

Banff

Tunnel Mountain Road

Tunnel Mountain Road

★ Hoodoos Lookout

Bow River

Banff Ave.

Tunnel Mountain Drive

Deer St.

Cougar St.

Moose St.

★ Banff Centre

St. Julien Road

Banff Ave.

Squirrel St.

Elk St.

Marten St.

St.

Wolf St.

Otter St.

Beaver St.

Mount Norquay Rd.

Lynx St.

Bow Ave

Caribou St.

Bear St.

Buffalo St.

Bow River

Bow River Falls

Spray Ave.

Glen Ave.

Bow River

Whyte Museum
of the Canadian Rockies

Birch Ave.

★ Buffalo Nations
Luxton Museum

★ Cascade Gardens

Kootenay Ave.

Banff Springs Hotel ★

Cave Ave.

Mountain Ave.

Cave and Basin Marsh

★ Cave and Basin
National Historic Site

© ULYSSE / ULYSSES

▲ The Banff Springs Hotel and its splendid surroundings.
© iStockphoto.com / InStock Photographic Ltd.

◀ Catharine Whyte, Rudolph Aemmer, Peter Whyte, and Neil Begg on the crest of Abbot Pass, 1930.
© Whyte Museum of the Canadian Rockies Collection

Aboriginal settlements, including clothing, tools and jewellery. They also learn about the history of certain local heroes and famous explorers like Bill Peyto, as well as that of the railway and the town of Banff. Personal effects and clothing that once belonged to notable local figures are exhibited. The museum also houses a painting gallery and extensive archives, for those who wish to learn more about the region.

Created in 1933, the **Banff Centre ★** is the home of the Banff Centre of the Arts. Every summer, this renowned cultural centre hosts the **Banff Arts Festival**, which attracts numerous artists in the fields of dance, opera, jazz and theatre.

The **Hoodoos Lookout ★★** is located just outside of the town of Banff. The hoodoos aren't as striking as those in Central Alberta's badlands, but they are

Their way of life, rituals and hunting techniques are explained, and various tools they used are displayed.

The **Whyte Museum of the Canadian Rockies ★★★** relates the history of the Canadian Rockies. Here, museumgoers will discover archaeological findings from ancient Kootenay and Stoney

definitely worth a look. Like gigantic stalagmites, these windswept pillars of sand, silt, gravel and dissolved limestone stand like sentinels guarding the surrounding forest.

Bow Valley Parkway ★ ★

To get from Banff to Lake Louise, travellers can take the Bow Valley Parkway, which weaves its way along the mountains and affords exquisite views of the Bow River. It is important to drive slowly here, as animals often approach the road at sunrise and sunset.

The Bow River Valley was first created by the torrential currents of the Bow River, which originated from the thaw flow of surrounding mountains some 140 million years ago. The river, which no longer depends on thaw flow, continued its journey across the glacial debris, progressively eroding the rock along the edge of the valley and giving it its rounded shape.

A stop at beautiful **Johnston Canyon ★ ★ ★**, located about 20km beyond Banff, is a must. A small dirt trail has been cleared through the canyon, where visitors can behold the devastat-ing effect even a small torrent of water can have on all kinds of rock. The first waterfall, called the Lower Falls, is only 1.1km along the trail, and the path here is easy, though a bit slippery in spots. The second, called the Upper Falls, lies another 2.7km farther. This canyon is a veritable bird sanctuary, and bird lovers can often spot some dippers here, as they live in the canyon year-round and like to dive into the icy waters in search of insect larvae. Black swifts also abound, as they build their nests in the shady hollows of the canyon. They arrive in mid-June and stay until the beginning of fall, long enough to raise their young before heading back south to the warmth of the tropics. The second waterfall is the canyon's highest, and this is where visitors can marvel at what are known as "shimmering walls." A sign explains the phenomenon, which results from the combination of several varieties of algae saturated with minerals. When the sun hits the wall the effect is spectacular. The trail continues over another 3km to the **Ink Pots**, which are formed by seven cold springs, in different shades of blue and green.

▼   The thundering waterfalls of Johnston Canyon. © *Philippe Renault*

LAKE LOUISE AND THE ICEFIELDS PARKWAY ★ ★ ★

Lake Louise ★ ★ ★

Jewel of the Canadian Rockies, the town of Lake Louise is known the world over thanks to its small, tranquil, emerald-green lake. Few natural sites in Canada can boast as much success: this little place welcomes an average of about 4.5 million visitors every year!

Lake Louise's popularity is nothing new, and visitors today owe its rediscovery (not discovery, since this area was already well known to Aboriginal people) to Tom Wilson, a railway surveyor for Canadian Pacific. In 1882, while working near the Pipestone River, Tom Wilson heard the rumbling of an avalanche coming from the Victoria Glacier. He proceeded to ask a Stoney Aboriginal named Nimrod to lead him to the "Lake of the Little Fishes," which is what the local native people called the lake. Struck by the colour of the water, Tom Wilson renamed the lake "Emerald Lake." It was subsequently renamed again, this time after Queen Victoria's daughter, Princess Louise Caroline Alberta, who also gave her name to the province of Alberta.

Though the present-day **Chateau Lake Louise ★ ★** (now known as the Fairmont Chateau Lake Louise) has nothing to do with the original building (1909), it remains an attraction in itself. This vast hotel can accommodate more than 1,100 visitors. Besides restaurants, the hotel houses a small shopping arcade with boutiques selling all kinds of gifts and souvenirs.

Visitors can take a stroll around Lake Louise or climb the mountain along the network of little trails that radiates out from the lake's shore to get a magnificent view of the Victoria Glacier, the lake and the glacial valley. Reaching **Lake Agnes ★ ★ ★** requires extra effort, but the view of the **Victoria** (3,464m), **Whyte** (2,983m), **Fairview** (2,111m), **Babel** (3,111m) and **Fay** (3,235m) mountains is well worth the exertion.

Moraine Lake ★ ★ ★

Though much smaller than Lake Louise, Moraine Lake is no less spectacular. Inaccessible in the winter as the road that leads to it is closed from mid-October to late May, the lake often remains frozen until June. Visitors should therefore be prepared for cool temperatures, even in summer. The Moraine Lake valley, known as the **"Valley of the Ten Peaks,"** was created by the **Wenkchemna Glacier**, which can still be found at the bottom of the valley. The 10 summits were originally named after the Assiniboine words for the numbers 1 to 10, but many have since been renamed, and only the appellation Wenkchemna (peak number 10) remains.

The Icefields Parkway ★ ★ ★

The Icefields Parkway follows Highway 93 from Lake Louise over some 230km to the Continental Divide, which is covered by glaciers, before ending up in Jasper. This wide, well-paved road is one of the busiest in the Rockies dur-

◀ Moraine Lake and the Valley of the Ten Peaks in Banff National Park. © *Travel Alberta*

Lake Louise and the Icefields Parkway

▲ The majestic landscape of Bow Summit.
© *Travel Alberta*

▶ Moraine Lake, an unforgettable vision of the untamed West. © *Philippe Renault*

ing the summer. It runs through some incredibly majestic scenery and is often crossed by wild animals.

The **Hector Lake** ★★ lookout, 16km from Lake Louise, offers a great view of both the lake and Mount Hector. The lake is fed by melt water from the Balfour Glacier and the Waputik Icefields.

Bow Summit ★★ (2,088m) lies at the highest point of the Icefields Parkway, on the Continental Divide. At this point the vegetation changes drastically, giving way almost completely to sub-alpine plant-life. By the side of the road is a rest area that overlooks **Peyto Lake** (pronounced *Pee-Toh*). Visitors can

Lake Louise and the Icefields Parkway

take a hike through this area of alpine vegetation, and if the weather is right, they can admire the lovely little lake. Curiously, the colour of the lake can vary considerably depending on the season. With the first signs of spring, it brightens to a marvellous metallic blue, which then becomes paler and paler as more and more sediment mixes with the water.

A lookout located 113km north of Lake Louise and 117km south of Jasper offers a view of the North Saskatchewan River and the magnificent **Bridal Veil Falls ★★**. Nearby is the **Castleguard Cave**, a network of underwater caves, the longest in Canada, that extends over 20km under the Columbia Icefield. Because of frequent flooding and the inherent dangers of cave exploration, visitors must obtain authorization from Parks Canada to enter the caves.

Athabasca Glacier ★ ★ ★

The focal point of the icefields tour, the Athabasca Glacier stands at 2,000m above sea level, 127km north of Lake Louise and 103km south of Jasper. Here, information panels show the impressive retreat of the glacier over the years:

1,6km over the last century alone. In fact, it is rather the glacier's size which has shrunk due to atmospheric warming. Those who wish to explore the ice on foot should be mindful of crevasses, which can be up to 40m deep. There are 30,000 on the Athabasca Glacier, some of which are hidden under thin layers of snow or ice.

The **Icefield Centre** is an enormous "green" building. Visitors should be sure not to miss the **Glacier Gallery ★ ★ ★**, a fascinating interactive exhibition which, through a variety of models, films and found objects, explains everything there is to know about the glaciers, in particular offering plenty of information on the past that has been preserved in the ice for over 10,000 years.

The **Stutfield Glacier ★ ★** lookout provides a view of one of the six huge glaciers that are fed by the Columbia Icefield, which continues one kilometre into the valley. About 3km farther, on the west side, are several avalanche corridors, some of which come right up to the road. Generally, however, park rangers trigger avalanches before the thick layers of snow become dangerous.

▼ The Icefields Parkway. © *Philippe Renault*

▲ The roaring waters of Sunwapta Falls. © *Travel Alberta*

▲ Athabasca Falls illuminates its surroundings with a rainbow.
    © *Travel Alberta*

▶ Majestic Mount Edith Cavell. © *Travel Alberta*

Fifty-five kilometres before Jasper, the **Sunwapta Falls ★ ★ ★** and canyon provide a good example of how water can work away at limestone. The countryside offers some typical examples of suspended valleys, which result when smaller glaciers attach themselves to larger ones. The valley left by the larger glacier is much deeper, and the shallower, smaller one appears suspended. Several hiking trails have been cleared, one of which leads to the base of the Sunwapta Falls. Visitors should be careful when hiking here, as this is one of the park's prime habitats for bears and moose.

The trail leading to the 23m high **Athabasca Falls ★ ★**, located about 25 kilometres farther along, takes about an hour to hike. The concrete structure built there is an unfortunate addition to the natural surroundings, but heavy traffic in the area would have otherwise destroyed the fragile vegetation. Furthermore, some careless visitors have suffered accidents because they got too close to the edge of the canyon. Travellers are therefore reminded not to go beyond the barriers.

Several hiking trails have been cleared to allow visitors to enjoy a better view of majestic **Mount Edith Cavell ★ ★ ★** (3,363m), as well as its suspended gla-

cier, the **Angel Glacier**. The mountain is named after Edith Louisa Cavell, a British nurse who became known in World War I for her refusal to leave her post near Brussels so that she could continue caring for the wounded on both sides. Arrested for spying by the Germans and accused of having helped Allied prisoners escape, she was shot on October 12th, 1915. To commemorate this woman's exceptional courage, the government of Canada decided to name the most impressive mountain in the Athabasca Valley after the martyred nurse.

JASPER NATIONAL PARK VIA THE YELLOWHEAD HIGHWAY ★ ★ ★

Jasper National Park ★ ★ ★

Covering 11,228km², Jasper National Park is the Canadian Rockies' largest park. It was created by the Canadian government in 1907.

The **Ashlar Ridge Viewpoint** ★ ★ offers a stunning view of the region. Nearby are the **Miette Hot Springs** ★ ★, the hottest springs in all of the Rockies' parks.

Jasper National Park via the Yellowhead Highway

Here, the sulphurous water gushes forth at 54°C and must be cooled down to 40°C for the baths.

Hiking trails have been cleared in **Maligne Canyon ★★★** so that visitors can admire this spectacular narrow gorge abounding with cascades, fossils and potholes sculpted by the turbulent waters. Several bridges span the canyon. The first offers a view of the falls; the second, of the effect of ice on rock; the third marks the gorge's deepest point.

Maligne Lake ★★ is one of the prettiest lakes in the Rockies. Water activities such as boating, fishing and canoeing are possible here, and a short trail runs

along part of the shore. The chalet on the shore houses a souvenir shop, a restaurant-café and the offices of a tour company that organizes trips to little **Spirit Island**, the ideal vantage point to admire the surrounding mountain tops.

Jasper ★

The town of Jasper takes its name from an old fur-trading post which was founded in 1811 by William Henry of the North West Company. Jasper is a small town of barely 5,000 residents which owes its tourist development to its geographic location and the train station that was built here in 1911. When the Icefields Parkway was opened in 1940, the number of visitors who wanted to

discover the region's majestic scenery just kept growing. Although this area is a major tourist draw, Jasper remains a decidedly more tranquil and less commercialized destination than Banff.

KOOTENAY NATIONAL PARK VIA THE OLD WINDEMERE HIGHWAY

Kootenay National Park ★ ★

Although less popular than Banff and Jasper, Kootenay National Park nevertheless boasts beautiful, majestic landscapes and is just as interesting to visit as its more touristy neighbours. It contains two large valleys, the humid Vermillion River Valley and the drier Kootenay River Valley; the contrast is striking. The park owes its existence to a bold attempt to lay a road between the Windermere region and the province of Alberta. In 1905, Randolphe Bruce, a businessman from the town of Invermere who became the lieutenant governor of British Columbia, decided to turn a profit with the local orchards. To accomplish this, he had to be able to transport produce to other parts of the country, hence the necessity of laying a road between isolated Windermere and the cities to the east. Bruce was so influential that construction began in 1911. A number of obstacles sprung up, and the audacious project soon proved too costly for the province to finance alone. The 22km of completed road, born of a bitter struggle between man and nature, ended up leading nowhere, and the project was abandoned. Refusing to admit defeat, Bruce turned to the federal government, which agreed to help in return for several hectares of property that lined the road on both sides; thus was born Kootenay National Park in 1922.

Vermilion Pass, at the entrance of Kootenay Park, marks the Continental Divide; from this point on, rivers in Banff Park and points east flow to the east, while those in Kootenay Park flow west and empty into the Pacific.

A few kilometres farther lies **Marble Canyon ★ ★**. Marble Canyon is very narrow, but visitors will find a lovely waterfall at the end of the 800m **Marble Canyon Trail**. Several bridges span the

The inspiring stillness of Maligne Lake.
© Philippe Renault

Kootenay National Park via the Old Windemere Highway

gorge, and the erosion caused by torrential waters makes for some amazing scenery.

Five hundred metres past the canyon, visitors will find a trail leading to the famous **Paint Pots ★**. These ochre deposits are created by subterranean springs which cause iron oxide to rise to the surface. Native people used this substance as paint. They would clean the ochre, mix it with water, and mould it into little loaves, which they would bake in a fire. They would then ground it into a fine powder and mix it with fish oil. They could use the final product to paint their bodies or decorate their tepees and clothing. According to the Aboriginals, a great animal spirit and a thunder spirit lived in the streams. Sometimes they would hear a melody coming from here, other times battle songs; according to their lore, this meant that the spirits were speaking to them. For these Natives, the ochre represented spirits, legends and important customs, while the first Whites who came here saw it as an opportunity to make money. At the beginning of the century, they extracted the ochre by hand and then sent it to Calgary to be used as a colouring for paint. You can still see a few remnants of this era, including machines, tools and even a few piles of ochre which were left behind when the area was made into a national park and all work here came to a halt.

Radium Hot Springs

The major attraction in Radium Hot Springs are the **Radium Hot Pools ★★**, whose warm waters are apparently renowned for their therapeutic virtues. Whether or not you believe these claims, which have yet to be backed by

any medical evidence, a soak in these 38°C non-sulphurous waters is definitely very relaxing.

FROM GOLDEN TO YOHO NATIONAL PARK ★★

Golden

The town of Golden is located on the Kicking Horse River, making it an ideal place for hiking. Residents and visitors can enjoy the trails on either side of the river, which are connected by the **Golden Bridge ★★★**, Canada's longest single span timber frame pedestrian bridge. The bridge was built in 24 days by around 100 volunteers from Canada, the United States and Europe.

Yoho National Park ★★

Hiking to **Emerald Lake ★★★** has become a tradition in Yoho National Park. A short trail (5.2km) takes hikers around the lake, who can then visit **Hamilton Falls ★★**. Picnic areas have been laid out near the lake, and a small canoe-rental outfit provides an opportunity to enjoy some time on the water.

Visitors must be accompanied by a guide to visit the **Burgess Shale ★★★**. In 1909, a paleontologist discovered several large trilobite beds on Mount Stephen, near Field. Since the Rockies were once covered by an ocean, all of these fossils were beautifully preserved by a thick layer of marine sediment. The invaluable fossil beds on Mount Burgess, beside Mount Stephen, were pushed to the surface by the geological upheavals that led to the emergence of the Rockies. Visitors will need to set

▲ Emerald Lake in Yoho National Park.
© *Philippe Renault*

▲ A trilobite fossil preserved in the Burgess Shale. © *Burgess Shale Geoscience Foundation*

▶ The waters of Yoho National Park.
© *Philippe Renaud*

aside an entire day to visit the Burgess Shale, since the trip there and back involves a 20km hike. To enlist the services of a guide, they should contact the park offices or the **Burgess Shale Geoscience Foundation** several days in advance.

A few kilometres past Field, **Yoho Valley Road** leads to Takakkaw Falls. On the way, travellers can stop at the **Upper Spiral Tunnel Viewpoint** ★ ★ to admire the advanced technology the engineers working for the railway company had to employ in order to lay a dependable line across this hilly terrain.

The small road twists and turns for 13km, leading to a wonderful scenic viewpoint from which visitors can contemplate the Yoho and Kicking Horse

Rivers. It comes to a dead end at the **Takakkaw Falls** ★ ★, among the highest in Canada.

CANMORE AND KANANASKIS VALLEY ★ ★

When Captain John Palliser led a British scientific expedition here from 1857 to 1860, the numerous lakes and rivers he found led him to christen the region Kanananaskis, which means "gathering of the waters." Located 90km from Calgary, this region covers more than 4,000km², including the Bow Valley,

Next pages

▶ One of the stunning views in the Kananaskis region. © *Travel Alberta*

Canmore and Kananaskis Valley

Bragg Creek and Peter Lougheed provincial parks. Because of its proximity to Calgary, its beautiful scenery and the huge variety of outdoor activities that can be enjoyed here, it soon became one of the most popular destinations in the Rockies.

Canmore ★

The name Canmore comes from the Gaelic *Ceann mor*, which means "big head." The name was given as a nickname to Scottish king Malcolm III, son of Duncan I, who became king in 1054 and established his place in history by killing the usurper Macbeth. After searching for the most practical route for the railway to the west, Canadian Pacific chose to go through the Bow Valley. It was decided that the supply station for the project would be placed

at the entrance to the Rockies, and thus was born the town of Canmore. Coal deposits found here later were mined until 1979.

Kananaskis Valley

Kananaskis Village consists mainly of a central square surrounded by two luxurious hotels. The region's leading resort, it was officially inaugurated in 1987, and its construction was funded by the Alberta Heritage Savings Trust and a number of private investors.

There are many ranches along the southern route that crosses the Kananaskis Valley. As they are passing through the area, travellers often encounter herds of cattle that seem quite at home in the middle road. Activities here include cart rides, rodeos and river rafting.

▼   Canmore and its landmark Three Sisters Mountain Range. © *Travel Alberta*

Calgary

Calgary ★ ★ is a thriving metropolis of concrete and steel, and a western city through and through. Set against the Rocky Mountains to the west and prairie ranch-lands to the east, this young, prosperous city flourished during the region's various oil booms, but its nickname, Cowtown, tells a different story. Before the oil, there were cowboys and gentlemen, and Calgary originally grew thanks to a handful of wealthy ranching families.

Over-grazed lands in the United States and an open grazing policy north of the border drew many ranchers to the fertile plains around Calgary. Wealthy English and American investors soon bought up land near Calgary, and once again Calgary boomed. The beginning of the 20th century was a time of population growth and expansion, only slightly jarred by World War I.

Oil was the next big ticket. Crude oil was discovered in Turner Valley in 1914 and Calgary was on its way to becoming a modern city. Starting in the mid-20th century, the population soared and construction boomed. As the global energy crisis pushed oil prices up, world corporations moved their headquarters to Calgary, and though the oil was extracted elsewhere, the deals were made here.

▼ Downtown Calgary, the metropolis of Alberta. © iStockphoto.com / Jess Wiberg

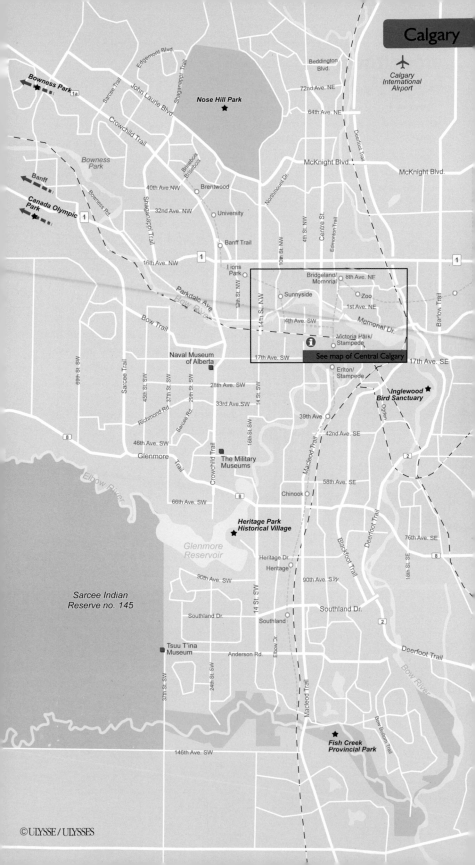

Calgary

Bowness Park

★ Banff

Canada Olympic
Park

Bowness Park

Edgemont Blvd.

John Laurie Blvd

Shaganappi Trail

Sarcee Trail

Crowchild Trail

Bowness Rd.

Shaganappi Trail

Beddington
Blvd.

72nd Ave. NE

Nose Hill Park ★

64th Ave. NE

Calgary
International
Airport

McKnight Blvd.

McKnight Blvd.

Brisebois
Brisebois

40th Ave NW

Brentwood

32nd. Ave. NW

University

Banff Trail

16th Ave. NW

Parkdale Ave

Bow River

Northmount Dr.

4th St. NW

Centre St.

Edmonton Trail

Deerfoot Trail

10th St. NW

Lions
Park

13th St. NW

14th St. NW

Sunnyside

Bridgeland/
Memorial

Zoo

1st Ave. NE

8th Ave. NE

4th Ave. SW

Memorial. Dr.

Barlow Trail

ⓘ

Victoria Park/
Stampede

See map of Central Calgary

Naval Museum
of Alberta

69th St. SW

Sarcee Trail

45th St. SW

37th St.

29th St. SW

Richmond Rd.

Sarcee Rd.

Crowchild Trail

28th Ave. SW

33rd Ave. SW

14th St. SW

16th St. SW

17th Ave. SW

Erlton/
Stampede

17th Ave. SE

Inglewood
Bird Sanctuary ★

Ogden

39th Ave.

42nd Ave. SE

46th Ave. SW

Glenmore

The Military
Museums

58th Ave. SE

Macleod Trail

Blackfoot Trail

Deerfoot Trail

18th St. SE

76th Ave. SE

66th Ave. SW

Chinook

Heritage Park
Historical Village ★

Glenmore
Reservoir

90th Ave. SW

Heritage Dr.

Heritage

90th Ave. SW

Sarcee Indian
Reserve no. 145

Southland Dr.

14 St. SW

Southland

Elbow Dr.

Southland Dr.

Tsuu T'ina
Museum

37th St. SW

24th St. SW

Anderson Rd.

Macleod Trail

Deerfoot Trail

Bow River

Bow Bottom Trail

Fish Creek
Provincial Park ★

146th Ave. SW

© ULYSSE / ULYSSES

DOWNTOWN ★★

The 190m, 762-step, 55-storey **Calgary Tower ★★** is the city's most famous landmark. It offers a breathtaking view of the city, including the ski-jump towers at Canada Olympic Park, the Saddledome and the Canadian Rockies, as well as a restaurant. Photographers should take note that the specially tinted windows on the observation deck make for great photos.

The stunning **Glenbow Museum ★★★** boasts three floors of permanent and travelling exhibits that chronicle the exciting history of Western Canada. The displays include contemporary and Aboriginal art, as well as an overview of the various stages of the settling of the West, from the First Nations to the first pioneers, the fur trade, the North West Mounted Police, ranching, oil and agriculture.

A peculiar looking concrete building is home to the **TELUS World of Science ★★★**, a wonderful museum that never fails to enchant children. The museum boasts a planetarium, an observatory, a science hall and two theatres that showcase mystery plays and special-effects shows.

◀ The entrance to the Glenbow Museum on Stephen Avenue. © *Travel Alberta*

▼ Historic re-enactment in Fort Calgary.
© *Fort Calgary*

Central Calgary

St. George Drive

Murdock Rd.

Zoo

St. George's Island

Calgary Zoo, Botanical Garden & Prehistoric Park

14th St.

13th St. SE

12th St. SE

12th Street Bridge

11th Ave. SE

12th St. NE

11A St. NE

11th St. NE

Bridgeland / Memorial

9th Ave. SE

9th St. SE

Deane House

1a

10th St.

9A St.

8th St. NE

2nd Ave.

McDougall Rd.

Murdock Rd.

St. Patrick Island

Maggie St.

Elbow River

7A St. NE

7th St. NE

6A St. NE

6th St. NE

Meredith

Marsh

Fort Calgary

9th Avenue Bridge

11th Ave. SE

12th Ave. SE

13th Ave. SE

Grain Academy

Pengrowth Saddledome

Radford Rd.

8th Ave. NE

7th Ave. NE

5th St. NE

Murdock Rd.

4th St. NE

6th St. SE

5th St. SE

Olympic Way

3rd St. NE

1st Ave. NE

Memorial Drive

4th St. SE

4th Ave. NE

Bow River

River Front Ave.

3rd St. SE

Macleod Trail

Olympic Way

14th Ave. SE

Stampede Park

7th Ave. NE

6th Ave. NE

5th Ave. NE

4th Ave. NE

3rd Ave. NE

2nd Ave. NE

5th Ave. SE

6th Ave. SE

City Hall

4th Ave. SE

5th Ave. SE

6th Ave. SE

Olympic Plaza

Glenbow Museum

10th Ave. SW

11th Ave. SW

14th Ave. SW

1st St. NE

Centre St. N

Chinatown

Centre St. S

Calgary Chinese Cultural Centre

Centre St. S

1st St. SW

Stephen Avenue Mall

Calgary Tower

2nd St. SW

1st St. SW

Crescent Rd.

Prince's Island Park

2nd Ave. SW

2nd St. SW

3rd St. SW

Devonian Gardens

4th St. SW

2nd St. SW

4th St.

4A St.

5th St.

5A St.

Eau Claire Market

Downtown

3rd Ave. SW

3rd St. SW

4th St. SW

4th Ave. SW

5th St. SW

13th St. SW

15th St. SW

7th St. NW

4th Ave. NW

Memorial Drive

1st Ave. SW

6th St. SW

6th Ave. SW

8th Ave. SW

9th Ave. SW

5th Ave. SW

6th St. SW

7th Ave. SW

8th Ave. SW

9th Ave. SW

Crescent Rd.

3rd Ave.

2nd Ave.

1st Ave.

Sunnyside

9th St.

8th St.

7th Ave. SW

8th Ave. SW

11th Ave. SW

12th Ave. SW

Victoria Park / Stampede

Kensington

Louise Bridge

4th Ave. SW

5th Ave. SW

6th Ave. SW

9th St.

8th Ave. SW

9th Ave. SW

10th Ave. SW

Southern Alberta Institute of Technology

10th St. NW

10A St. NW

11th St. NW

11A St. NW

12th St. NW

13th St. NW

Kensington Rd.

Gladstone Road

TELUS World of Science

Mewata Armory

11th Ave. SW

12th St SW

13th Ave. SW

14th Ave. SW

5th Ave. NW

Bow River

© ULYSSE / ULYSSES

ALONG THE BOW RIVER ★ ★ ★

Fort Calgary ★ ★ ★ was built as part of the March West, which brought the North West Mounted Police to the Canadian West to stop the whisky trade. "F" Troop arrived at the confluence of the Bow and Elbow rivers in 1875, and chose to set up camp here. Nothing remains of the original Fort Calgary, and the fort will never be completely rebuilt as that would interfere with archaeological work already underway. An excellent interpretive centre includes great hands-on displays, woodworking demonstrations and the chance to try on the famous scarlet Mountie uniform. Friendly guides in period costumes provide tours.

The **Calgary Zoo, Botanical Garden & Prehistoric Park** ★ ★ opened in 1920 and is known for its realistic re-creations of natural habitats, now home to over 300 species of animals. The Botanical Garden boasts some 10,000 plants and trees, while the Prehistoric Park recreates the world of dinosaurs with a collection of full-size replicas set amidst plants and rock formations from prehistoric Alberta.

SOUTHEAST AND SOUTHWEST ★

The Southeast is Calgary's industrial area, but it is also the site of the "Greatest Outdoor Show on Earth," the Calgary Stampede. At the intersection of Ninth Avenue SE and the Bow lies

A POT OF BLACK GOLD

Almost 400 million years ago, great coral reefs formed along the Pacific coast, in what is now eastern Alberta. After the reefs died, the coral fossilized into porous rock. Billions of marine organisms lived and died above and within this coral. Their remains accumulated at the ocean floor in the cavities of the fossilized coral. One hundred million years ago, the Pacific retreated to what are today the foothills of the Rockies. Naturally, the watercourses on the newly revealed plains flowed into the ocean. With time, they in turn deposited a layer of sediment that would become tight rock over the layer of porous rock. Nature had just put the lid on a tremendous pot where carbon matter, subjected to the right pressure and temperature, slowly began to change. Hundreds of millions of years later, the contents of this pot would become Alberta's fortune: oil.

▶   Calgary's skyscrapers tower over the Saddledome.
© Travel Alberta

THE GREATEST OUTDOOR SHOW ON EARTH!

The **Calgary Stampede** began in 1912, at a time when many people expected that the wheat industry would eventually supersede the cattle industry. It was originally intended to be a one-time showcase for traditional cowboy skills. Of course, the cattle industry thrived and the show has been a huge success ever since. Every July, some 100,000 people descend on Stampede Park for the extravaganza.

It begins with a parade, which starts at the corner of Sixth Avenue SE and Third Street SE. Visitors need to get there early (by 7am) if they want to see anything. The main attraction is the rodeo where cowboys and cowgirls show off their skills and vie for nearly one million dollars in prize money. The trials take place every afternoon and the big final is held on the last weekend.

At Stampede Park, the Grandstand Show is a non-stop musical variety spectacular. Evening performances often showcase some of the biggest stars in country music.

▼ A cowboy and his horse leap into the ring. © *Travel Alberta*

▲ The Heritage Park Historical Village offers a window on history. © *Travel Alberta*

the **Inglewood Bird Sanctuary** ★★, a good spot for strolling and bird-watching.

Visitors who are in town in July during the **Calgary Stampede** can get out their Stetson, hitch up their horse and get ready for a rompin' good time. The festivities take place at **Stampede Park** and the aptly named **Pengrowth Saddledome**, which has the world's largest cable-suspended roof and is a giant testimony to the city's cowboy roots.

In Southwestern Calgary, **17th Avenue SW**, also known as "Uptown 17th," is home to boutiques, cafés and restaurants. This lively thoroughfare is located in the heart of the **Mission District**, where the area's earliest settlement was established by Catholic missionaries in the 1870s, when it was known as Rouleauville. West of the Mission District is the ritzy **Mount Royal** neighbourhood, where luxurious residences face the Elbow River.

Fish Creek Provincial Park ★★ lies south of the city. The largest urban park in Canada, it boasts trails that lead walkers, joggers and cyclists through stands of aspen and spruce, prairie grasslands and floodplains dotted with poplar and willow trees. An abundance of wildflowers can be found in the park, as can mule deer, white-tailed deer and coyotes. An interpretive trail, artificial lake and beach, playground, picnic areas and a restaurant are some of the park's facilities.

Heritage Park Historical Village ★★ is a 26ha park on the Glenbow Reservoir. Visitors can step back in time as they stroll through a real 1910-era town that features historic houses decorated with period furniture, wooden sidewalks, a working blacksmith, a tipi, an old schoolhouse, a post office, a divine candy store and the Gilbert and Jay Bakery, known for its sourdough bread. Staff in period dress play piano in the houses and take on the role of

Southeast and Southwest

THE RODEO

Rodeos are serious business in Alberta. In some schools, cowboy skills are part of the sports program and are on a par with football and hockey.

There are essentially six official events in a rodeo. In the bareback riding, saddle bronc riding, and bull riding events, the cowboy must stay on the bucking animal for eight seconds to even qualify, at which point he is given a score based on style, rhythm and control. In bareback and saddle bronc riding, the animal is a horse, and in all three cases a cinch is placed around the animal's hind quarters which causes him to buck. The bull riding event is of course the most exciting, with the bulls weighing over 800kg.

In the calf roping event the cowboy must lasso the calf from his horse, race to the animal and tie three of its legs. This is a timed event, and the time includes a final six seconds during which the calf must remain tied. Big cowboys are the usual participants in the steer wrestling event where the cowboy slides off his horse onto the steer, grabs its horns, twists them and throws the steer to the ground. Once again, the fastest time wins.

The barrel racing event is the only one for cowgirls. Riders must circle three barrels in a clover-leaf pattern, and there is a five-second penalty for knocking one over. Other entertaining events and rodeo clowns keep the crowd happy in between the official events. One of the most amusing crowd-pleasers is mutton busting, where young cowpokes are strapped to sheep and sent flying around the corral.

suffragettes speaking out for women's equality in the Wainwright Hotel. Other areas in the park recreate an 1880s settlement, a fur trading post, a ranch, a farm and the coming of the railroad. Not only is this a magical place for children, with rides in a steam engine and a paddlewheeler boat on the reservoir, but it is also a relaxing place to escape the city and enjoy a picnic.

NORTHEAST AND NORTHWEST ★

North of the Bow River, the biggest draws in Northwest Calgary are Canada Olympic Park, Nose Hill Park and Bowness Park; Northeast Calgary has grown considerably in recent years and now has many hotels and restaurants, in addition to the airport.

Canada Olympic Park ★★★, or COP, built for the 1988 Winter Olympic Games, lies on the western outskirts of Calgary. This was the site of the ski-jumping, bobsleigh, luge, freestyle skiing and disabled events during the games, and it is now a world-class facility for training and competition. Artificial snow keeps the downhill ski slopes busy all winter.

Nose Hill Park ★ has an area of 1,127ha. This windswept hill rises 230m and is covered with native grasses and a few bushes. There is a handful of pretty hiking trails.

Bowness Park has always been a favourite escape for Calgarians. Visitors can paddle around its pretty lagoons in the summer, while in the winter they freeze up to form the city's largest skating rink.

BIRTHPLACE OF THE BLOODY CAESAR

Few people realize that the Bloody Caesar was invented right here in Calgary in 1969 by a man named Walter Chell, when he was beverage manager at the Calgary Inn (now the Westin Calgary Hotel). Not only did Chell invent the cocktail, but he was the brains behind its main ingredient as well, a combination of mashed clams and tomato juice, which he called clamato juice. You can even check with the company that later patented the juice as to its true origins.

Others have tried to copy, change and even take credit for Chell's recipe, but true Caesar drinkers know that 1.25 ounces of vodka, 5 ounces of Clamato juice and 3 dashes of Worcestershire sauce, all seasoned with salt, pepper and celery salt and garnished with a celery stalk combine to make the real thing!

Southern Alberta

Southern Alberta boasts some of the best sights and scenery in the whole province, from Waterton Lakes National Park and the mining towns of Crowsnest Pass to the historic native gathering place at Head-Smashed-In Buffalo Jump and the edge of the endless prairies.

The vast expanses and sometimes desert-like conditions that visitors traverse while making their way from west to east in Southern Alberta are in stark contrast to the looming, snow-capped Rocky Mountains to the west. Neat rows of wheat and other grains, perfectly round bales of hay, and the occasional grain elevator are about the extent of the relief across the slow-rolling terrain of this part of the province.

In Southern Alberta, visitors get to meet many descendants of immigrants—settled for several generations—from Europe, the United States and other parts of the world. There was a time when, for people from countries other than those of the West, acceptance was difficult. In the 19th century, experience

© Travel Alberta

in farming was a determining factor for the Canadian immigration program, but the racial ideas of the time also had an influence on which were considered desirable and undesirable ethnic groups. As a result, the British and the Americans, who often arrived in Southern Alberta in groups riding in covered wagons, were at the top of the list of desirable immigrants according to the Immigration Directorate.

▼ The scenic route through Waterton Lakes National Park. © Travel Alberta

Southern Alberta

SOUTHERN FOOTHILLS ★★

Longview

The **Bar U Ranch National Historic Site ★★★** commemorates the contribution of ranching to the development of Canada. Until recently still a working ranch, it is one of four ranches that once covered almost all of Alberta. Parks Canada and Canadian Heritage now administer the ranch, working with the Friends of the Bar U Ranch. Visitors can wander freely around the ranch and observe ranching operations, although these are staged. "Bar U" refers to the symbol that was branded on cattle from this ranch. A beautiful visitor centre features an interpretive display on breeds of cattle, roundup techniques, branding and quirt whips. A 15min video on the *Mighty Bar U* conveys the romance of the cowboy way of life and also explains how the native grasslands and Chinook winds unique to Alberta have been a perpetual cornerstone of ranching. The centre also houses a gift shop and a restaurant where visitors can taste an authentic buffalo burger.

Crowsnest Pass ★

The area along Highway 3 between Pincher Creek and the continental divide is known as the Municipality of Crowsnest Pass. A number of once thriving coal-mining communities along the highway are now home to a handful of sites offering an interesting historical perspective on the local mining industry. Coal was first discovered here in 1845, but it wasn't until 1898, when the Canadian Pacific Railway built a line through the pass, that the area was really settled. Coal was the only industry, and when the mineral turned out to be inferior in quality and hard to extract, troubled times set in. Local coal fetched lower prices than that of British Columbia, and by 1915 the first mine had closed; the others soon followed. The municipality was declared a Historic District in 1988.

The **Bellevue Mine ★★** opened in 1903 and had been operating for seven years without incident when it was rocked by an underground explosion on December 9, 1910. Afterdamp poisoning lead to the deaths of 30 min-

ers. The mine eventually reopened and remained operational until 1962. Today, visitors are given hard hats and miner's lamps and get to follow a guided tour through some 100m of dark, cool and damp underground mine tunnels. This is the only mine in the Pass open to visitors and is a real treat for both young and old.

Continuing along Highway 3, travellers will notice a drastic change in the landscape. Extending on both sides of the highway and covering 3km², the debris

of the Frank Slide creates a spectacular, almost lunar landscape. Consisting mostly of limestone, the boulders are on average 14m deep, but exceed 30m in some places. The **Frank Slide Interpretive Centre ★★**, located north of the highway on a slight rise, presents an audiovisual account of the growth of the town and of the slide itself. It explains the various theories about what caused the landslide on April 29, 1903 that sent 82 million tonnes of limestone crashing from the summit of Turtle Mountain onto the town of Frank, which

▼   Bar U Ranch National Historic Site, a scene from the past.   © *Travel Alberta*

Frank Slide Interpretive Centre and Turtle Mountain. © *Travel Alberta*

at the time lay south of the highway at the foot of the mountain. All that remains of the town is an old fire hydrant. The mountain's unstable structure, mining, water and severe weather are believed to have contributed to the disaster. A self-guided trail through the slide area provides an interesting perspective of its scope. Sixty-eight of the town's residents were buried, but the disaster might have been worse if it hadn't been for a Canadian Pacific brakeman who, amazingly, raced across the rocks to stop an approaching passenger train. Those who dare can set out on a trail

An angler at Crowsnest Pass. © *Travel Alberta*

THE CHINOOK WIND

A Chinook occurs when moisture-laden winds from the Pacific Ocean strike the Rocky Mountains and are forced to precipitate their moisture as rain or snow. This leaves the winds cold and dry. However, as the air descends the eastern slopes, it remains dry but is condensed by the increase in atmospheric pressure and warms up. This warm, dry wind brings mild conditions that can melt 30cm of snow in a few hours. It is essentially because of the Chinook that Alberta's native grasses survive the winter and that cattle can graze on the prairies year-round. The warm, dry breath of the Chinook is a fabled part of Alberta history. It is the stuff of legend, with stories of farmers rushing home at the sight of the telltale Chinook arch (an arch-shaped cloud formed when the air pushes the cloud cover to the west), with their horses' front legs in snow and hind legs in mud!

that climbs Turtle Mountain to examine fissures and cracks near the summit that still pose a threat.

Waterton Lakes National Park ★ ★ ★

Waterton Lakes National Park forms one half of the world's first International Peace Park, the other half being Glacier National Park, in Montana (U.S.A.). Waterton boasts some of the best scenery in the province and is well worth a side trip. Characterized by a chain of deep glacial lakes and mountains with irregularly shaped summits, this area where the peaks meet the prairies offers wonderful hiking, cross-country skiing, camping and wildlife-watching opportunities. The unique geology of the area consists of 1.5-billion-year-old sedimentary rock from the Rockies that was dumped on the 60-million-year-old

▲ Wild animals refresh themselves in Waterton Lakes National Park. © *Travel Alberta*

shale of the prairie during the last ice age. Hardly any transition zone exists between these two regions, which are home to abundant and varied wildlife; species from a prairie habitat mix with those of sub-alpine and alpine regions (some 800 varieties of plants and 250 species of birds). One thing to remem-

Southern Foothills

▲ The Remington Carriage Museum, for a ride into the old days. © *Travel Alberta*

▸ Head-Smashed-In Buffalo Jump Interpretive Centre. © *Travel Alberta*

ber, and visitors are reminded of it as they enter the park, is that the wild animals here are just that—wild. While they may appear tame, they are unpredictable and potentially dangerous, and visitors are responsible for their own safety.

Cardston ★

Cardston is a prosperous-looking town nestled in the rolling foothills where the grasslands begin to give way to golden fields of wheat and of canola. The town was established by Mormon pioneers fleeing religious persecution in Utah. Their move here marked one of the last great covered-wagon migrations of the 19th century. Cardston might not seem like much of a tourist town, but it is home to one of the most impressive monuments and one of the most unusual museums in Alberta. The monu-

ment is the **Cardston Alberta Temple**, which seems a tad out of place rising from the prairie. This truly majestic edifice took 10 years to construct and was the first temple built by the Mormon Church outside the United States.

The museum is the **Remington-Alberta Carriage Centre ★★★**, opened in 1993. Though a carriage theme may seem narrow for a museum, this one is definitely worth a visit. Forty-nine of the more than 300 carriages were donated by Don Remington of Cardston on the condition that the Alberta government build an interpretive centre in which to display them. The wonderfully restored carriages and enthusiastic, dedicated staff at this magnificent facility make this exhibit first-rate. Visitors can take a guided tour through the $1,675m^2$ display gallery, where town mock-ups and animated street scenes provide

Southern Foothills

the backdrop for the collection, one of the world's best elite carriage facilities. The interesting documentary *Wheels of Change* tells the story of this once huge industry, which was all but dead by 1922. Visitors can also learn how to drive a carriage, watch the restoration work in progress, take a carriage ride and have an old-fashioned picture taken.

Head-Smashed-In Buffalo Jump ★★★

The arrival of the horse in the mid-1700s signalled the end of a traditional way of hunting buffalo among Plains Indians. For 5,700 years before this, the Plains Indians had depended on the Head-Smashed-In Buffalo Jump. From it

they got meat, both fresh and dried for pemmican; hides for tipis, clothing and moccasins; and bones and horns for tools and decorations. Head-Smashed-In was an ideal spot for a jump, with a vast grazing area to the west. The Plains Indians would construct drive lines with stone cairns leading to the cliff. Some 500 people participated in the yearly hunt, during which men dressed in buffalo-calf robes and wolf skins would lure the herd towards the precipice. Upon reaching the cliff, the leading buffalo were forced over the edge by the momentum of the stampeding herd behind them. The herd was not actually chased over the cliff, but were rather driven to a panic that would lead to a stampede. The area remains much as it was thousands of years ago, though the distance from the cliff to the ground drastically changed as the bones of butchered bison piled up, 10m deep in some places.

LETHBRIDGE TO MEDICINE HAT ★★

Lethbridge ★★

Lethbridge, known affectionately by locals as "downtown L.A.," (for *Lethbridge, Alberta*) is Alberta's fourth largest city, and a pleasant urban oasis on the prairies. Steeped in history, the city boasts an extensive park system, pretty tree-lined streets, interesting sights and a diverse cultural community. Visitors are as likely to meet ranchers as business people, Hutterites or Mormons on the streets of *L.A.*

◀ The picturesque tipi campground at Head-Smashed-In Buffalo Jump. © *Travel Alberta*

Lethbridge to Medicine Hat

▲ Fort Whoop-Up Interpretive Centre, Indian Battle Park. © *Travel Alberta*

▸ Nikka Yuko Japanese Garden. © *Travel Alberta*

Indian Battle Park ★★, in the Oldman River valley in the heart of town, is where Lethbridge's history comes alive; it is the site of Fort Whoop-Up, the setting of a terrible battle. On October 25, 1870, Cree, displaced by European settlers into Blackfoot territory attacked a band of Blood Blackfoot camped on the banks of the Oldman River. In the ensuing battle, the Blood were aided by a group of Peigan Blackfoot nearby; by the end, some 300 Crees and 50 Blackfoots were dead.

Paths weave their way through five traditional Japanese gardens at the **Nikka Yuko Japanese Garden** ★★. These aren't bright, flowery gardens, but simple arrangements of green shrubs, sand and rocks in the style of a true Japanese garden—perfect for quiet contemplation. Created by renowned Japanese garden designer Dr. Tadashi Kudo of the Osaka Prefecture University in Japan, Nikka Yuko was built in 1967 as a centennial project and a symbol of Japanese and Canadian friendship (*Nikka Yuko* actually means friendship). The bell at the gardens symbolizes this friendship, and when it is rung good things are believed to happen simultaneously in both countries.

Milk River

The Milk River is the only river in Western Canada on the east side of the continental divide that does not eventually empty into Hudson Bay; it flows south into the Missouri River and on into the Mississippi River and the Gulf of Mexico. As a result, the area has been claimed by eight different governments and countries. When France claimed all lands that drained into the Mississippi, this part of Alberta was under French jurisdiction. The Spanish, the British, the Americans, and the Hudson's Bay Company have all staked their claim at some point in history.

Lethbridge to Medicine Hat

Writing-on-Stone Provincial Park ★★

When approaching Writing-on-Stone Provincial Park, on can't help but notice the carved-out valley of the Milk River and, in the distance, the Sweetgrass Hills rising up in the state of Montana. The Milk River lies in a wide, green valley with strange rock formations and steep sandstone cliffs. The hoodoos, formed by iron-rich layers of sandstone that protect the softer underlying layers, appear like strange mushroom-shaped formations. These formations, along with the cliffs, were believed to house the powerful spirits of all things in the world, attracting Aboriginal people to this sacred place as many as 3,000 years ago. Writing-on-Stone Provincial Park protects some fascinating petroglyphs (rock carvings) and pictographs (rock paintings), with some dating back to 1,800 years ago. Precise dating of the rock art is difficult and based solely on styles of drawing and tell-tale objects; for example, horses and guns imply that the drawings continued into the 18th and 19th centuries, while some works seem to date from the Late Prehistoric Period.

ACROSS THE PRAIRIE TO MEDICINE HAT ★★

The prairies roll on and on as far as the eye can see along this stretch of highway surrounded by golden fields that are empty but for the occasional hamlet, grain elevator or abandoned farmhouse. Towns were set up every 16km because that was how far a farmer could haul his grain.

▶ Some of the rock art in the park. © *Travel Alberta*

▼ Writing-on-Stone Provincial Park. © *Travel Alberta*

▲ Cypress Hills Interprovincial Park, straddling Alberta and Saskatchewan. © *Travel Alberta*

Medicine Hat ★

Rudyard Kipling once called Medicine Hat *"a city with all hell for a basement,"* in reference to Medicine Hat's location above some of western Canada's largest natural gas fields. The town prospered because of this natural resource, which now supplies a thriving petrochemical industry. Clay deposits nearby also left their mark on the city, contributing to its once thriving pottery industry. Medicine Hat, like many towns in Alberta, boasts several parks. As for its name, legend has it that a great battle between the Cree and the Blackfoot took place here. During the battle, the Cree medicine man deserted his people and, while fleeing across the river, lost his headdress in mid-stream. Believing this to be a bad omen, the Cree aban-

doned the fight, and were massacred by the Blackfoot. The battle site was called *Saamis*, which means medicine man's hat. When the Mounties arrived years later, the name was translated and shortened to Medicine Hat.

Cypress Hills Interprovincial Park ★★

Cypress Hills Interprovincial Park is Alberta's second largest provincial park and the only interprovincial park in the province. This wooded oasis of lodgepole pine rises out of the prairie grassland and harbours a varied wildlife, including deer, moose and some 215 species of birds (including wild turkeys). At least 18 species of orchid also thrive in the park; some bloom throughout the summer, but the best time to see

them is mid-June. There are, however, no cypress trees in the park; the French word for lodgepole pine is *cyprès*, and the name *montagnes de cyprès* was mistranslated to Cypress Hills.

This was also the site of the Cypress Hill Massacre. Two American whisky-trading posts were established in the hills in the early 1870s. During the winter of 1872-3, some Assiniboine were camped in the hills, close to these two posts, when a party of drunken American hunters, whose horses had been stolen, came upon the band of Assiniboine. Believing that they had taken the horses, the American hunters killed 20 innocent Assiniboine. The incident contrib-uted to the establishment of the North West Mounted Police to restore order. Three hundred Mounties arrived at Fort Walsh, Saskatchewan, and the men responsible for the massacre were arrested. Though they were not convicted because of lack of evidence, the fact that white men had been arrested gave credence in the eyes of the Aboriginal people to this new police force.

The park is rarely very busy, which provides visitors with an opportunity to enjoy great hiking and fishing in a peaceful environment. They can also rent boats or bicycles and play golf in summer, and go downhill skiing or spend a day tobogganing in winter.

Across the Prairie to Medicine Hat

Next page

▶ Between the mountains and the plains, in the heart of Alberta. © *Travel Alberta*

Central Alberta

A region that holds an inestimable amount of natural resources, Central Alberta encompasses a vast swath of the province that includes the Canadian Badlands, the foothills, the Rocky Mountains Forest Reserve and the heartland.

Where the Red Deer River Valley now lies was once the coastal region of a vast inland sea; its climate probably resembled that of the Florida Everglades and it was an ideal habitat for dinosaurs.

After the extinction of the dinosaurs, ice covered the land. As the ice retreated 10,000 years ago, it carved deep trenches in the prairie; this and subsequent erosion have uncovered dinosaur bones and shaped the region's fantastic landscape of hoodoos and coulees.

A part-Iroquois trapper and guide, Pierre Bostonais arrived in the West around 1800 as an employee of the Hudson's Bay Company. The light colour of his hair (when compared to his fellow workers) quickly earned him the nickname *Tête Jaune* (Yellowhead) among

French trappers. He led expeditions throughout the north of what are today Alberta and British Columbia, and followed the Smoky, Athabasca and Fraser rivers. He also crossed the Yellowhead Pass and established his famous cache of fur in a place now known as Tête Jaune Cache, at the junction of highways 5 and 16 (the Yellowhead Highway, which also bears his nickname). Bostonais was eventually killed by the Beaver, an Aboriginal people, in 1827.

▼   Dinosaur Provincial Park, heaven for palaeontologists. © *Travel Alberta*

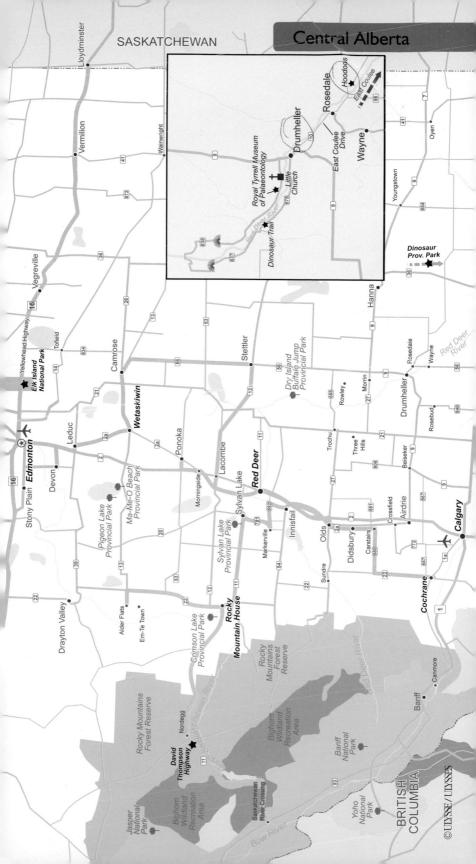

Lloydminster

Vermilion

Wainwright

Vegreville

Tofield

Elk Island
National Park

Yellowhead Highway

Stony Plain

Edmonton

Devon

Leduc

Camrose

Wetaskiwin

Ponoka

Lacombe

Red Deer

Sylvan Lake

Morningside

Markerville

Innisfail

Sundre

Olds

Didsbury

Carstairs

Crossfield

Airdrie

Cochrane

Calgary

Canmore

Banff

Banff
National Park

Yoho
National Park

BRITISH
COLUMBIA

Drayton Valley

Alder Flats

Em-Te Town

Crimson Lake
Provincial Park

Rocky
Mountain House

Nordegg

David
Thompson Highway

Saskatchewan
River Crossing

Jasper
National Park

Rocky Mountains
Forest Reserve

Bighorn
Wildland
Recreation
Area

Bighorn
Wildland
Recreation
Area

Rocky
Mountains
Forest
Reserve

Sylvan Lake
Provincial Park

Pigeon Lake
Provincial Park

Ma-Me-O Beach
Provincial Park

Stettler

Dry Island
Buffalo Jump
Provincial Park

Rowley

Morrin

Trochu

Three
Hills

Beiseker

Rosebud

Drumheller

Rosedale

Wayne

Red Deer
River

Hanna

Youngstown

Oyen

Dinosaur
Prov. Park

Rosedale

Hoodoos

East Coulee
Drive

East Coulee

Wayne

Drumheller

Royal Tyrrell Museum
of Palaeontology

Little
Church

Dinosaur Trail

Red Deer River

© ULYSSE / ULYSSES

DIGGING FOR DINOSAUR BONES

The very nature of the Red Deer River Valley means that every time it rains, more dinosaur bones are uncovered. The Royal Tyrrell Museum organizes various digs for budding palaeontologists, but you may just make a discovery of your own if you visit the area.

Any items found on the surface and on private land can be kept with the land-owner's permission. You can keep what you find as a custodian (ownership ultimately resides with the Province of Alberta), but you cannot sell the fossil or take it out of the province without permission.

Furthermore, fossils should never be removed from their original stratigraphic position without first mapping out that position, and you need a permit to excavate fossils. These treasures are an important part of the planet's history and should be treated as such.

DIGGING FOR DINOSAUR BONES AND OTHER TREASURES ★ ★ ★

Dinosaur Provincial Park ★ ★ ★

Dinosaur Provincial Park offers amateur palaeontologists the opportunity to walk through the land of the dinosaurs. Declared a UNESCO World Heritage Site in 1979, this nature preserve harbours a wealth of information on these formidable former inhabitants of the planet. Today, the park is home to more than 35 species of animals. A loop road and two self-guided trails (the **Cottonwood Flats Trail** and the **Badlands Trail**) provide a good summary introduction to the park. Two exposed dinosaur skeletons left where they were discovered can also be viewed.

Drumheller ★ ★ ★

The main attractions in Drumheller are located along the Dinosaur Trail and the Hoodoo Trail (see below); they include the Royal Tyrrell Museum of Palaeontology and the famous hoodoos. Erosion in the Red Deer River Valley has uncovered dinosaur bones

▲   One of the recreated animals in the Royal Tyrrell Museum of Palaeontology. © *Travel Alberta*

and shaped the fabulously interesting landscape of hoodoos and coulees found in Drumheller. Besides the bones, early settlers also discovered coal, though agriculture and the oil and gas industries now drive the local economy.

Dinosaur Trail ★ ★ ★

The gigantic **Royal Tyrrell Museum of Palaeontology ★ ★ ★** contains over 80,000 specimens, including 50 full-size dinosaur skeletons, as well as hands-on exhibits and multimedia presentations. The Royal Tyrrell is also a major

research centre, and visitors can watch scientists cleaning bones and preparing specimens for display.

Hoodoo Trail ★ ★ ★

Some of the most spectacular **hoodoos ★ ★ ★** in central Alberta can be found about halfway between Rosedale and East Coulee. These strange mushroom-shaped formations were created when the softer underlying sandstone eroded.

Digging for Dinosaur Bones and Other Treasures

The spectacular hoodoos along the Hoodoo Trail. © *Travel Alberta*

Man of Vision, an equestrian statue of Matthew Cochrane. © *Travel Alberta*

CENTRAL FOOTHILLS ★

Cochrane ★

The friendly town of Cochrane lies on the northern edge of Alberta's ranch-lands and was the site of the first big cattle ranch in the province. Ranching is still a part of the local economy, but

more and more Cochrane residents now commute into nearby Calgary, just 20min away, to earn their living.

The **Cochrane Ranche Provincial Historic Site ★★** commemorates the establishment in 1881 of the Cochrane Ranche Company by Québec business-man Senator Matthew Cochrane, and the birth of Alberta's cattle industry. The company controlled 189,000ha of sweeping grasslands which, along with three other ranches including the Bar U Ranch, covered most of Alberta.

Rocky Mountain House

Despite its evocative name, Rocky Mountain House is not a picturesque log cabin in the woods but rather a gateway town into the majestic Rocky Mountains.

The **Rocky Mountain House National Historic Park ★★** is interesting be cause it exemplifies, perhaps better than any other historic site, the inextric-able link between the fur trade and the discovery and exploration of Canada.

Central Foothills

David Thompson Highway ★★★

The road that leads to Rocky Mountain House runs along the edge of the Rocky Mountain Forest Reserve. As travellers approach the city, stunning views of the Rocky Mountains line the horizon. Highway 11, the David Thompson Highway, continues west from Rocky Mountain House up into the Aspen Parkland and on into Banff National Park.

THE HEARTLAND ★

Red Deer ★

During the Riel Rebellion of 1885, the Canadian militia built Fort Normandeau on the present site of Red Deer. The post was later occupied by the North West Mounted Police. The railway, agriculture, oil and gas industries all contributed to the growth of Red Deer, at one point the fastest growing city in Canada.

Fort Normandeau ★ as it stands today is a replica of the original. A stopping house next to the river was fortified and enclosed in palisade walls by the Carabiniers de Mont Royal regiment under Lieutenant J.E. Bédard Normandeau in anticipation of an attack by the Cree during the Louis Riel Rebellion of 1885.

◀ Rocky Mountain House National Historic Site. © *Travel Alberta*

▼ The idyllic countryside along the David Thompson Highway. © *Travel Alberta*

DAVID THOMPSON

David Thompson began at the Hudson's Bay Company in 1784 as a clerk stationed at several posts on Hudson Bay and the Saskatchewan River. While laid up with a broken leg, he took an interest in surveying and practical astronomy. After years of exploring and surveying much of present-day northern Manitoba and Saskatchewan, he decided to switch camps and go to work for the North West Company in 1797. The company enlisted his services in the "Columbia Enterprise," the search for a route through the Rockies.

In 1806-07, Thompson made preparations to cross the Rockies at Rocky Mountain House. However, the Peigan First Nation, who frequented the post, opposed the project; if trade extended west of the Rockies, their enemies, the Kootenay and Flathead, would acquire guns. Thompson thus moved up-river from Rocky Mountain House to the Howse Pass in 1807.

In 1810, the race to the mouth of the Columbia came to a head when news of an American expedition reached Thompson. He immediately headed west but was blocked by the Peigan. He headed north again, skirting Peigan territory. In 1811, he crossed the Athabasca Pass and reached the mouth of the Columbia River on the Pacific Ocean a few months after the Americans had set up their post there.

Thompson later settled in Terrebonne, near Montréal, and worked on the establishment of the boundary between Upper and Lower Canada. He was unsuccessful in business and died in 1857, in poverty and virtual obscurity.

Wetaskiwin

The city of Wetaskiwin is home to one of the finest museums in the province. Much like the province's other regional museums, the Reynolds-Alberta Museum proves again that there is more to Alberta than Calgary, Edmonton and the Rockies. Though there isn't much to see in Wetaskiwin, this pleasant city has an interesting main street and respectable restaurants and hotels, and the museum is definitely worth the trip in itself.

The **Reynolds-Alberta Museum** ★ ★ ★ celebrates the "spirit of the machine" and is a wonderful place to explore, with its interactive displays for children that bring everything to life. A top-notch collection of restored automobiles, trucks, bicycles, tractors and farm machinery is on display. Among the vintage cars is one of about 470 Model J Duesenberg Phaeton Royales. This one-of-a-kind automobile cost $20,000 when it was purchased in 1929! Visitors to the museum will also learn how a grain elevator works, and can observe the goings-on in the restoration workshop through a large picture window.

THE YELLOWHEAD ★ ★

The scenic **Yellowhead Highway** follows Highway 16 west from Winnipeg, Manitoba and across the prairies through Saskatoon, Saskatchewan, before reaching the Alberta border at Lloydminster. It then crosses Alberta, passing the provincial capital, Edmonton, and Jasper, in the Rockies. Once in British Columbia it splits, heading south on Highway 5 to

Central Foothills

Merritt and continuing on Highway 16 west all the way to Prince Rupert.

Elk Island National Park ★ ★

Magnificent Elk Island National Park preserves part of the Beaver Hills area as it was before the arrival of settlers when Sarcee and Plains Cree hunted and trapped in these lands. This island wilderness in a sea of grass preserves two herds of bison, plains bison and the rare wood bison. The park offers some of the best wildlife viewing in the province, as it is also home to moose, deer, lynx, beavers and coyotes. It is also crossed by major migratory flyways, with trumpeter swans often passing by in the fall.

◀ Visiting the past at the Reynolds-Alberta Museum. © *Reynolds Alberta Museum*

▼ Elk Island National Park and its observation walkway. © *Travel Alberta*

Next page

▶ The skyline of Edmonton, capital of Alberta. © *Travel Alberta*

Edmonton

Edmonton ★★ seems to suffer from an image problem, and undeservedly so. People have trouble getting past the boomtown atmosphere and the huge mall! Admittedly it is a boomtown: a city that grew out of the wealth of the natural resources that surround it. But this city has grown to become one of the world's largest northerly cities, encompassing an attractive downtown core, Canada's largest urban parks system and numerous cultural facilities, including theatres and many festivals.

The region had long been frequented by Aboriginal peoples who searched for quartzite to make tools and trapped the area's abundant beaver and muskrat. It was precisely this supply of fur that attracted traders to the area in the late 18th century. The Hudson's Bay Company established Fort Edmonton in 1795 next to the North West Company's Fort Augustus overlooking the North Saskatchewan River, where the Legislative Building now stands. Edmonton's fortunes rose and fell over the following years, until the next boom, when merchants tried to attract Klondike Gold Rush prospectors so they would pass through Edmonton on their way to Dawson City.

Agriculture remained the bread and butter of Alberta's capital until the oil well at Leduc blew in. Since then, Edmonton has been one of Canada's fastest growing cities.

DOWNTOWN AND NORTH OF THE RIVER ★ ★

The **River Valley Parks** system lies along the North Saskatchewan River and consists of several small parks where you can bicycle, jog, go swimming, play golf or just generally enjoy the natural surroundings. The amount of land set aside for parks per capita is higher in Edmonton than anywhere else in the country.

With its impressive eight-storey glass pyramid designed by local architect Gene Dub, Edmonton's **City Hall** is the centrepiece of the **Downtown Arts District**. It is not the only exceptional building in the area, though. The **Francis Winspear Centre for Music ★ ★** is faced with Tyndall limestone and bricks to match the city hall. Built with a $6 million gift from Edmonton businessman Francis Winspear, the 1,900-seat hall is considered an acoustic won-

▲ The River Valley Parks, blue and green spaces for outdoor recreation. © *Travel Alberta*

◄ City Hall, with its pyramid and clock tower.
© *Travel Alberta*

The Francis Winspear Centre for Music, home of the Edmonton Symphony Orchestra. © *Travel Alberta*

der and as a result, attracts a wide range of musicians. It is now the home of the Edmonton Symphony Orchestra.

The **Art Gallery of Alberta** ★★ boasts an extensive collection of Canadian and contemporary art, complemented by various temporary exhibits.

In true Canadian Pacific tradition, the Château-style **Hotel Macdonald** ★★ is Edmonton's ritziest place to stay and was for many years the meeting place for members of Edmonton's high society. Completed in 1915 by the Grand Trunk Railway, it was designed by Montréal architects Ross and MacFarlane. The hotel had a brush with the wrecker's

The imposing Hotel Macdonald, like an imported European château. © *Travel Alberta*

Central Edmonton

Princess Elizabeth Ave.

111A Ave.

111th Ave.

110A Ave.

110th Ave.

109A Ave.

109th Ave.

108th Ave.

Kingsway Ave.

114th Ave.

113th Ave.

112th Ave.

Norwood Blvd.

110A Ave.

110th Ave.

109A Ave.

109th Ave.

108A Ave.

108th Ave.

107A Ave.

107th Ave.

106A Ave.

Clark Park

Ukrainian Canadian Archives & Museum of Alberta

Ukrainian Museum of Canada

St. Josaphat Ukrainian Catholic Cathedral

108th Ave.

107th Ave.

106th Ave.

105th Ave.

105th Ave.

104th Ave.

103A Ave.

103rd Ave.

106th Ave.

105th Ave.

104th Ave.

103A Ave.

103rd Ave.

102A Ave.

102nd Ave.

106th Ave.

105A Ave.

105th Ave.

104th Ave.

103A Ave.

103rd Ave.

City Hall

Art Gallery of Alberta

Churchill

Francis Winspear Centre for Music

Jasper Ave.

Rowland Rd.

102nd Ave.

Corona

Bay

Jasper Ave.

100th Ave.

99th Ave.

Grandin

98th Ave.

River Valley Parks

River Valley Rd.

Fortway Dr.

Hotel Macdonald

Grierson Hill

Low Level Bridge

James Macdonald Bridge

98th Ave.

Muttart Conservatory

Connors Rd.

Heritage Trail

98th Ave.

97th Ave.

Bellamy Hill Rd.

Scona Rd.

Alberta Legislature Building

High Level Bridge

105th Street Bridge

North Saskatchewan River

93rd Ave.

92nd Ave.

91st Ave.

90th Ave.

Rutherford House

John Walter Museum

University

89th Ave.

88th Ave.

Walterdale Rd.

Fort Hill

Saskatchewan Dr.

89th Ave.

88th Ave.

87th Ave.

87th Ave.

86th Ave.

85th Ave.

84th Ave.

83rd Ave.

G&E 1891 Railway Museum

86th Ave.

OLD STRATHCONA

Old Strathcona Farmer's Market

Whyte Ave. (82nd Ave.)

81st Ave.

80th Ave.

University Ave.

79th Ave.

78th Ave.

Calgary Trail

Gateway Blvd.

81st Ave.

80th Ave.

79th Ave.

78th Ave.

77th Ave.

WAYNE GRETZKY AND THE EDMONTON OILERS

The Oilers and three other World Hockey Association (WHA) teams joined the NHL in time for the 1979-80 hockey season. The Oilers were a well-managed, young team that knew how to scout recruits from the minor leagues. The team's owner even declared that his team would win the Stanley Cup (the trophy awarded to the winner of the finals) within five years or less. This was a bold prediction in a league where the championship title passed back and forth between the dynasties of the Montréal Canadiens and the New York Islanders.

▲ Statue of Wayne Gretzky at Rexall Place. © *Tourism Edmonton*

But while those teams were ageing, the Oilers were building their future. Their captain, Wayne Gretzky, soon earned the nickname "The Great One" due to his incredible natural talent. He accumulated record after record, and even scored five goals in one game on December 30, 1981. That day, he became the first player in hockey history to score 50 goals in such a short period of time: 39 games. He ended the season with 92 goals and 120 assists, an unprecedented record.

However, Oilers fans had to wait until their players matured, and it was not until 1984 that the Oilers finally broke the domination of the New York Islanders, who had just won four consecutive championships. The rest is history: the Oilers won five Stanley Cups in seven years, broke numerous records and had the satisfaction of winning the coveted trophy again in 1990, while Gretzky had been playing for the Los Angeles Kings for two years.

Having broken every imaginable record, Wayne Gretzky retired from competition in 1999. He is now the head coach of the Phoenix Coyotes (NHL). After toying with the idea of renaming their town "Gretzkyville," Edmonton instead decided to name a street after him, and the former Capilano Drive became Wayne Gretzky Drive. And why not?! The roads can turn to ice on cold winter days in Alberta's capital city!

ball in 1983 when it closed. A $28-million restoration, however, brought the Macdonald back in all its splendour.

Visitors can follow the tree-lined **Heritage Trail ★★★** to get from the Hotel Macdonald to the Alberta Legislature Building. This historic furtraders' route from Old Town to the site of Old Fort Edmonton is a 30min walk that follows the river bank for most of its length. A red-brick sidewalk, antique light standards and street signs help keep visitors on the right track. The river views along Macdonald Drive are remarkable, especially at sunset.

The 16-storey vaulted dome of the Edwardian **Alberta Legislature Building ★★** is a landmark in Edmonton's skyline. Sandstone from Calgary, marble from Québec, Pennsylvania and Italy, and mahogany from Belize were used to build the seat of Alberta's government in 1912. At the time, the Legislature stood next to the original Fort Edmonton. Today, it is surrounded by gardens and fountains.

OLD STRATHCONA AND SOUTH OF THE RIVER ★★

Once an autonomous city, Strathcona was founded when the Calgary and Edmonton Railway Company's rail line ended here in 1891. Brick buildings from that era still remain in this historic district, which is the best-preserved in Edmonton. While the area north of the North Saskatchewan River is clean, crisp and new with the unfinished feel of a boomtown, south of the river, in **Old Strathcona ★★★**, a sense of character is much more tangible. Here an artistic, cosmopolitan and historic atmosphere prevails.

▼ The Alberta Legislature Building at dusk, with its gardens and fountains. © *Travel Alberta*

GREATER EDMONTON ★★

The four glass-pyramid greenhouses of the **Muttart Conservatory ★★★** are another important landmark in Edmonton's skyline. Flourishing beneath three of these pyramids are floral displays of arid, temperate and tropical climates, respectively. Every month a new, vivid floral display is put together under the fourth pyramid.

West of downtown and north of the river is the **Royal Alberta Museum ★★**. The museum's collection traces the natural and human history of Alberta from the Cretaceous period through the Ice Age, and includes a display of pictographs by the province's earliest Aboriginal peoples. One highlight is the Syncrude Gallery of Aboriginal Culture, which explores the 11,000-year history of Aboriginal people in an interesting multimedia exhibit. The habitat gallery reproduces Alberta's four natural regions while the Bug Room is abuzz with exotic live insects.

Also north of the river is the **TELUS World of Science ★**, a recently expanded science museum which offers all sorts of fascinating interactive exhibits that never fail to entertain. Visitors can discover how their bodies work through 3-D models or solve a crime

▼   The glass pyramids of the Muttart Conservatory. © *Travel Alberta*

▲ Interior view of the immense West Edmonton Mall. © *Fallsview | Dreamstime.com*

▲ The scale model of the *Santa María*. © *West Edmonton Mall*

WEST EDMONTON MALL

What lies behind the walls of the West Edmonton Mall? There are real submarines at the Deep-Sea Adventure; the world's largest indoor amusement park; a National Hockey League–size rink where the Edmonton Oilers occasionally practise; an 18-hole miniature golf course; a waterpark complete with wave pool, waterslides, rapids, bungee jumping and whirlpools; a casino, bingo room and North America's largest billiard hall; fine dining on Bourbon Street; a life-size, hand-carved and painted replica of Columbus's flagship, the *Santa María*; replicas of England's crown jewels; a solid ivory pagoda; bronze sculptures; fabulous fountains, including one fashioned after a fountain at the Palace of Versailles; and, finally, the Fantasyland Hotel, a lodging option that truly lives up to its name...and we almost forgot, there are also some 800 shops and services—this is a mall after all!

▲ Fort Edmonton Park, for a trip back through time. © *Travel Alberta*

by collecting clues and analysing them in a lab. They can even explore all aspects of space exploration or experience the science of sport.

In the North Saskatchewan River Valley lies **Fort Edmonton Park ★★★**. Canada's largest historic park, it boasts an authentic reconstruction of Fort Edmonton as it stood in 1846. Four historic villages recreate different periods at the fort: the fur-trading era at the fort itself; the pre-railway era on 1885 Street; the municipal era on 1905 Street; and the postwar era on 1920 Street. Period buildings, period dress, period automobiles and period shops, including a bazaar, a general store, a saloon and a bakery, take visitors back in time.

Last, but certainly not least, is Edmonton's pride and joy, the **West Edmonton Mall ★★★**, the world's largest shopping and amusement complex.

Greater Edmonton

Northern Alberta

This vast hinterland offers excellent opportunities for outdoor pursuits as well as the chance to discover some of Alberta's cultural communities. Distances are so great, however, that touring the whole region is inconceivable unless you have all sorts of time and a car. The following tours explore the northern frontiers of Alberta, passing major attractions along the way.

Northern Alberta is home to a large French-speaking population; across the province, over 200,000 Albertans speak French. The first descendants of Europeans to settle permanently on the rich Alberta soil were French-speakers mainly from Québec, who had often come by way of the United States. In 1982, to demonstrate their French character, Franco-Albertans adopted a tricolour flag (blue, white and red) sporting a fleur-de-lis and Alberta's wild rose.

The Peace River area in Northwest Alberta is the youngest region of the province and the area with the largest percentage of Francophones. It is home to municipalities such as Donnelly and McLennan, French-speaking in spite of their typically English names. Immediately north of Edmonton is St. Albert, while northeast of the capital is St. Paul, the former Métis colony founded by Father Albert Lacombe in 1896, and Lac La Biche, in the heart of a lake region that once was a centre of commerce and fur trading and where the French community played a major role in Albertan history.

NORTHEAST TO COLD LAKE

Fort Saskatchewan

Established by the North West Mounted Police in 1875, Fort Saskatchewan, overlooking the North Saskatchewan River, was demolished in 1913, when it was taken over by the city of Edmonton. The **Fort Saskatchewan Museum** takes visitors back in time to the old town.

It features nine buildings dating from 1900 to 1920, including the original courthouse, a schoolhouse, a country church, a blacksmith's shop and an old log farm. Fort Saskatchewan became an independent city in 1985.

Smoky Lake

A Methodist mission was established on the present-day location of the **Victoria Settlement Provincial Historic**

▼   Historic family fun at Fort Saskatchewan. © *Travel Alberta*

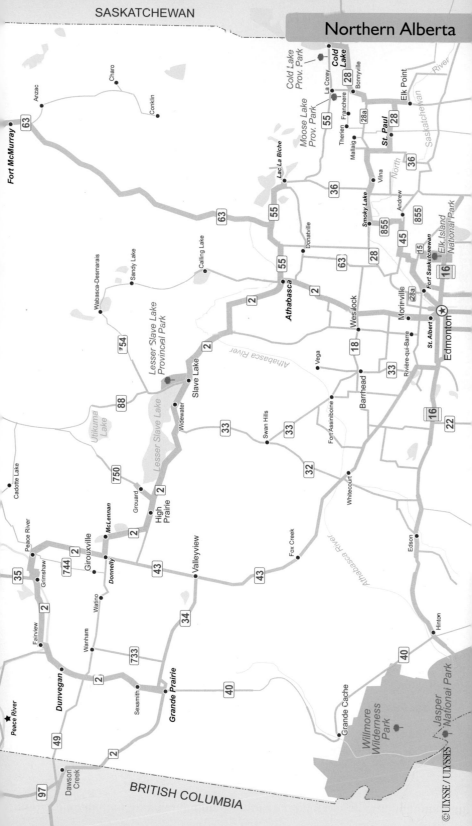

SASKATCHEWAN

Northern Alberta

Fort McMurray

Anzac

Charo

Conklin

Cold Lake

Cold Lake Prov. Park

La Corey

Bonnyville

Franchere

Therien

Moose Lake Prov. Park

Elk Point

St. Paul

Lac La Biche

Mallaig

Vilna

Andrew

Smoky Lake

Donatville

Westlock

Morinville

St. Albert

Edmonton

Fort Saskatchewan

Elk Island National Park

North Saskatchewan River

Athabasca

Vega

Rivière-qui-Barre

28a

Wabasca-Desmarais

Sandy Lake

Calling Lake

Barrhead

Cadotte Lake

Utikuma Lake

Lesser Slave Lake Provincial Park

Slave Lake

Widewater

Swan Hills

Fort Assiniboine

Athabasca River

Grouard

McLennan

High Prairie

Whitecourt

Edson

Girouxville

Peace River

Grimshaw

Donnelly

Valleyview

Fox Creek

Athabasca River

Hinton

Fairview

Watino

Wanham

Grande Prairie

Sexsmith

Grande Cache

Willmore Wilderness Park

Jasper National Park

Peace River

Dunvegan

Dawson Creek

BRITISH COLUMBIA

© ULYSSE / ULYSSES

▲ Sailboats moored on Cold Lake.
© *Travel Alberta*

hoping to attract Metis from all over Western Canada. Only 300 Metis, who had been continuously ignored by the government, responded to his invitation. Eventually settlers from a variety of cultural backgrounds arrived. The **St. Paul Historical Museum** examines the area's diverse cultural background. The **Old St. Paul Rectory** is located nearby.

Cold Lake

Home to Canadian Forces Base Cold Lake, this town actually relies on the nearby oil sands for its economic well-being. The nearby town of Medley is really just the post office, while Grand Centre is where all the shops are. The lake is the seventh largest in the province with an area of 370 km^2. Its name is fitting when you consider that its surface remains frozen for five months of the year. Its 100m depths attract fishers who come here to catch northern pike, walleye and trout.

NORTH OF EDMONTON ★

St. Albert ★ ★

Just north of Edmonton lies the community of St. Albert, the oldest farming settlement in Alberta. It began as a small log chapel in 1861, built by the Mary Immaculate Mission and Father Albert Lacombe. Born in Québec in 1827, Albert Lacombe began his missionary work in the former city of St. Boniface, now a part of Winnipeg, Manitoba. He convinced Bishop Alexandre Taché of

Site ★ in 1862, and two years later the Hudson's Bay Company set up Fort Victoria to compete with free traders at the settlement. This wonderfully peaceful spot along the Saskatchewan River, once a bustling village, was also the centre of a Metis community. The town was called Pakan, after a Cree chief who was loyal to the Riel Rebellion. When the railway moved to Smoky Lake, all the buildings were relocated; only the clerk's quarters were left behind. Exhibits and trails point out the highlights of this once thriving village that has all but disappeared.

St. Paul ★

The town of St. Paul was founded in 1896 when Father Albert Lacombe established a Metis settlement here

WOOD BUFFALO NATIONAL PARK ★ ★

Wood Buffalo National Park is accessible from the communities of Fort Chipewyan, Alberta, and Fort Smith, Northwest Territories. The park is home to the largest, free-roaming, self-regulating herd of bison in the world; it is also the only remaining nesting ground of the whooping crane. These two facts contributed to Wood Buffalo being designated a UNESCO World Heritage Site.

The park was initially established to protect the last remaining herd of wood bison in northern Canada. But when plains bison were shipped to the park between 1925 and 1928, due to overgrazing in Buffalo National Park in Wainwright, Alberta, the plains bison interbred with the wood bison, causing the extinction of pure wood bison. Or so it was thought. A herd was discovered in Elk Island National Park, some of which were shipped to Mackenzie Bison Sanctuary in the Northwest Territories. As a result, there are actually no pure wood buffalo in Wood Buffalo National Park.

Visitors who make the trip to the park can enjoy hiking (most trails are in the vicinity of Fort Smith), excellent canoeing and camping facilities, as well as the chance to experience Canada's northern wilderness in the country's largest national park.

▼   The traces of time in Wood Buffalo National Park. © *Travel Alberta*

the need for a mission dedicated to the Metis population, and St. Albert thus came into existence.

Father Lacombe only stayed at the new mission for four years, and then continued his work throughout the prairies. Bishop Vital Grandin moved his headquarters to St. Albert in 1868 and brought a group of skilled Oblate Brothers with him, making St. Albert the centre of missionary work in Alberta. Grandin played an important role in lobbying Ottawa for fair treatment of Aboriginal people, Metis and French Canadian settlers.

▼   Father Lacombe Chapel in St. Albert.
© iStockphoto.com / Jason Kasumovic

The **Heritage Musem** ★ is located in an interesting, contoured brick building called St. Ann Place. The museum houses an exceptional exhibit of artifacts and objects related to the history of the first citizens of St. Albert, including the Metis, First Nations people, missionaries and pioneers.

Athabasca ★

The town of Athabasca is located near the geographic centre of Alberta. The Athabasca River, which flows through the town, was the main corridor to the north, and the town of Athabasca was once a candidate for provincial capital.

The town was known as a jumping-off point for traders and adventurers heading north, and to this day, it is still a good starting point for outdoor adventurers as it lies right on the fringe of the northern hinterland, yet is only 1.5hrs north of Edmonton. Athabasca is also home to Athabasca University, Canada's most northerly university, reputed for its distance-education programs.

Lac La Biche

Lac La Biche (lake) is located on a divide separating the Athabasca River system, which drains into the Pacific, and the Churchill River system, which drains into Hudson Bay. Portage La Biche was a vital link on the transcontinental fur-trading route and was used by voyageurs to cross the 5km between Beaver Lake and Lac La Biche.

Fort McMurray ★ ★

Fort McMurray was developed around the Athabasca oil sands, the largest single oil deposit in the world. The oil is

ATHABASCA

The town began as Athabasca Landing, a Hudson's Bay Company trading post, and a point along one of the river trails that led north. Traders and explorers headed west on the North Saskatchewan River to present-day Edmonton, then overland on a hazardous 130km portage, cut in 1823, to the Athabasca River at Fort Assiniboine, southwest of the present-day town of Athabasca. It was this pitiful trail that spelt disaster for Klondikers in 1897-98 on the "All-Canadian Route" from Edmonton.

A new trail, the Athabasca Landing Trail, was created in 1877. It soon became the major highway to the north and a transshipment point for northern posts and the Peace River. Hudson's Bay Company scows built in Athabasca were manned by a group known as the Athabasca Brigade, composed mainly of Cree and Metis. This brigade handily guided the scows down the Athabasca River through rapids and shallow waters to points north. Most scows were disassembled on arrival and used as building materials, but those that returned had to be pulled again by the brigades. Paddlewheelers eventually replaced these scows.

actually bitumen, a heavy oil whose extraction requires an expensive, lengthy process; the deposits consist of compacted sand mixed with the bitumen. The sand is brought to the surface, where the bitumen is separated and treated to produce a lighter, more useful oil. The one trillion barrels of bitumen in the sands promise a vital supply for future energy needs.

The **Fort McMurray Oil Sands Discovery Centre** ★★ explains the extraction process, and much more, through colourful hands-on exhibits.

PEACE RIVER VALLEY ★

McLennan

This small town located on the edge of Lake Kimiwan proudly claims the title of "Bird Capital of Canada," and it's easy to

▲ The northern lights illuminate the sky above Fort McMurray. © *Travel Alberta*

◄ Complete serenity envelops the Peace River. © *Travel Alberta*

see why. Three major migratory flyways converge here, giving bird-watchers the chance to observe over 200 different

species. The town has an interesting interpretive centre and boardwalk that leads to a bird blind.

Peace River ★ ★

The mighty Peace River makes its way from British Columbia's interior to Lake Athabasca in northeastern Alberta. Fur trappers and traders used the river to get upstream from Fort Forks to posts at Dunvegan and Fort Vermillion. Fort Forks was established by Alexander Mackenzie in 1792 where the town of Peace River now stands. Mackenzie was the first person to cross what is now Canada and reach the Pacific Ocean. Exceptional scenery greets anyone who visits this area, and legend has it that anyone who drinks from the Peace River will someday return.

Dunvegan ★

With Alberta's longest suspension bridge as a backdrop, **Historic Dunvegan ★** peacefully overlooks the Peace River. Once part of the territory of the Dunne-za (Beaver) First Nation, this site was chosen in 1805 for a North West Company fort, later a Hudson's Bay Company fort. Dunvegan became a major trade and provisioning centre for the Upper Peace River and later the Hudson's Bay headquarters for the Athabasca district. By the 1840s Catholic missionaries were visiting Dunvegan, including a visit by the eminent Father Albert Lacombe in 1855. In 1867, the Catholic St. Charles Mission was established, and was joined in 1879 by the Anglican St. Savior's Mission, making Dunvegan a centre for missionary activity.

Peace River Valley

▼ Nineteenth-century log buildings in Historic Dunvegan. © *Travel Alberta*

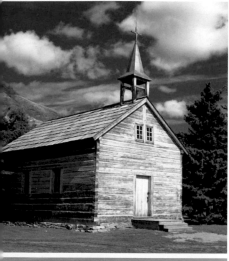

Grande Prairie ★

As Alberta's fastest growing city, Canada's forest capital and the Swan City, Grande Prairie is a major business and service centre in northern Alberta, thanks to natural gas reserves in the area. The town is so named because of *la grande prairie*, highly fertile agricultural lands that are exceptional this far north. Unlike most towns in Alberta's north, Grande Prairie is not what was left behind when the trading post closed. From the start, homesteaders were attracted to the area's fertile farmland.

The landmark design of **Grande Prairie Regional College**, with its curved red brick exterior, is the work of Alberta Aboriginal architect Douglas Cardinal, who also designed Gatineau, Québec's Canadian Museum of Civilization.

◄ The beautiful natural setting of Grande Prairie Regional College. © *Travel Alberta*

▼ Grande Prairie and its limitless rich farmland. © *Travel Alberta*

Saskatchewan

In the popular imagination, Saskatchewan is nothing but one continuous wheat field, a place with little topography or cultural diversity. And the traveller passing through parts of southern Saskatchewan in late summer can hardly be forgiven for thinking otherwise: this is Canada's breadbasket, after all, producing a full 60% of the nation's wheat in acres of golden fields that literally stretch to the horizon.

It is for this reason that the place is usually portrayed as nothing more than a cold monotonous patch of grassland between the lakes of Manitoba and the mountains of Alberta. And it's true: the entire province is subject to such bitterly cold winters that "plug-ins"—electric connections that keep a car battery warm overnight—are standard at a good hotel.

However, a little probing reveals a much richer identity than the stereotype suggests. The spectacular Qu'Appelle River Valley cuts across the level plain with deep glacial creases running down to the river, while a venture through Saskatchewan's two major

cities, Saskatoon and Regina, reveals surprising architectural touches. In other areas, a preponderance of Eastern European churches crop up—painted church domes rising from the prairie like delicately painted Easter eggs, testifying to the province's solid Ukrainian influence.

Farther north, the prairies abruptly give way to foothills and then genuine mountains, woods and lakes. There is in fact more forest in Saskatchewan—half a province worth, in fact—than farmland. Most of the major rivers in the province flow east into Manitoba, eventually emptying into Hudson Bay.

▼ A beautiful sea of yellow flowers in a canola field. © *iStockphoto.com / Andrew David*

NORTHWEST
TERRITORIES

Saskatchewan

MANITOBA

ALBERTA

Lake
Athabasca

Reindeer
Lake

Lynn Lake

Fort
McMurray

63

Southend

Lac La Ronge
Provincial Park

La Ronge

La Ronge
Lake

Flin Flon

106

Medley

Meadow Lake

Narrow Hills
Provincial Park

The Pas

Bonnyville

St. Paul

Prince Albert
National Park

Cumberland House
Provincial Historic Park

Vermilion

Lloydminster

3

The Battlefords
Provincial Park

55

Nipawin

Lake
Winnipegosis

Wainwright

16

North Battleford

Battleford

Fort Battleford
National
Historic Site

Hafford

Borden

Fort Carlton
Prov. Hist. Park

40

Duck
Lake

Redberry
Lake

Prince Albert

St Laurent
Shrine

Batoche National
Historic Site

Melfort

368

Greenwater
Prov. Park

3

Consort

21

29

Saskatoon

St.Brieux

11

2

20

Muenster

5

Little Quill
Lake

Kelvington

9

Swan River

14

Little Manitou
Lake

Wadena

Biggar

Pike Lake
Prov. Park

Big Quill
Lake

16

8

Oyen

Kindersley

11

365

Watrous

Simpson

Last Mountain Lake
National Wildlife Area

35

310

Canora

Kamsack

47

Veregin

Yorkton

Wroxton

Last Mtn.
Lake

20

Qu'Appelle River

Last Mountain House
Prov. Historic Park

320

22

Motherwell Homestead
National Historic
Site

10

47

Melville

22

247

201

Crooked
Lake

16

Buffalo

Fort Qu'Appelle

10

1

Grenfell

Round
Lake

Medicine Hat

Moose Jaw

Regina

Crooked Lake
Provincial Park

Whitewood

Swift Current

363

339

Claybank

Cannington Manor
Provincial Historic Park

1

19

58

43

Lethbridge

Cypress Hills
Interprovincial Park

13

Eastend

18

58

13

Gravelbourg

Willow Bunch

Weyburn

13

9

6

13

Val Marie

Grasslands
National Park

Wood Mtn.
Post Prov. Park

39

NORTH DAKOTA
(UNITED STATES)

MONTANA
(UNITED STATES)

©ULYSSE / ULYSSES

REGINA ★

Named in honour of Queen Victoria, the city of Regina was founded in 1903. The province's capital and second largest city after Saskatoon, Regina is the cultural and commercial centre of Saskatchewan.

Though it's hard to see from downtown, the **Wascana Centre ★★★** is a huge green space—reputedly the largest urban park in North America; even larger than New York City's Central Park—and the logical spot from which to begin exploring the city. This nearly 400ha complex includes a lake, a university, bridges, lawns, gardens, a convention centre and even a bird sanctuary. Walking trails and bike paths wind throughout.

Saskatchewan's cruciform **Legislative Building ★★★**, facing Wascana Lake and landscaped gardens and lawns, may be Canada's most impressive provincial capital building. Its huge dome rises above the city; at the entrance, the fountain is one of a pair from London's Trafalgar Square (the other is now in Ottawa).

▼ Wascana Lake. © iStockphoto.com / Lauri Wiberg

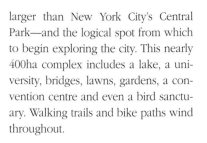

▼ Regina's Legislative Building and its flower gardens. © Tourism Saskatchewan, J.F. Bergeron

Pages 204-205

▶ Spectacular view of a Saskatchewan golf course. © Tourism Saskatchewan, Douglas E. Walker

Regina

Victoria Park ★★★ is an outstanding urban green space, the best on the prairies, right in the centre of Regina with a fantastic view of downtown's modern skyscrapers. A series of pathways radiate like spokes of a wheel outward from the war memorial at the centre; spruce trees add a lovely contrast to the grass and gardens.

SOUTHERN SASKATCHEWAN

The Trans-Canada Highway runs east to west through southern Saskatchewan, crossing wheatfields and the occasional town. East of Regina, it gives no hint of the spectacular vista lying just a few kilometres to the north, in the Qu'Appelle River Valley, which runs parallel to it at this point. West of

▼ An isolated chapel in the Qu'Appelle River Valley. © *Tourism Saskatchewan, Douglas E. Walker*

Regina the land is perfectly flat; this is the scenery for which Saskatchewan is best known, making humans feel, as the popular saying goes, like a fly on a plate.

Qu'Appelle River Valley ★ ★ ★

The Fort Qu'Appelle River Valley makes for a surprising detour: the river has cut a little valley in the otherwise flat countryside. Route 247 (north of the Trans-Canada between Whitewood and Grenfell), barely known by tourists, runs along the river as it dips through the brown and green hills. It passes **Round Lake ★ ★** and then **Crooked Lake Provincial Park ★ ★**, beautiful lakes for swimming, fishing and sightseeing. A string of tiny tree-shaded resort towns provides campgrounds and the odd country store.

▲   Grasslands National Park. © *Tourism Saskatchewan, Douglas E. Walker*

Southern Saskatchewan

Grasslands National Park ★ ★

Grasslands National Park was the
first representative portion of original
mixed-grass prairie set aside in North
America. Among the variety of habitats represented here are grasslands,
buttes, badlands and the Frenchman
River Valley; spectacular views can be
enjoyed from some of the butte tops,
while the wildlife includes the rare
swift fox, pronghorn antelopes, bur-
rowing owls, and golden eagles. Most
interesting, though, is the unique prairie dog town, where colonies of black-
tailed prairie dogs still live in their natural environment.

Moose Jaw

The secret underground passages of
Moose Jaw were but a rumour until
a car plunged through the pavement
and wound up 4m below street level
in what are now referred to as the
Tunnels of Moose Jaw ★ ★ ★. Today,
visitors can take two guided tours of
the newly renovated underground
passageways. During the *Passage to
Fortune* tour, interpreters explain how
they were built by the Chinese labour-
ers who had come to work on the railway and decided to go "underground,"
in this case literally, when Canada
went back on its promise to grant them

▲ A whooping crane.
© Tourism Saskatchewan

citizenship once the task was completed. The tour evokes the abysmal living conditions endured by the Chinese in these dark, cramped quarters.

You'd better bring along your tommy gun for the second tour, "The Chicago Connection." The tunnels were later used as hideouts of a different kind, as bootlegging operations were set up here and gangsters from as far away as Chicago slipped into town, evading the long arm of the law. Guides in period costumes—and attitudes—take visitors through this 1920s bootlegging operation with a twist.

Last Mountain Lake National Wildlife Area ★ ★

The Last Mountain Lake National Wildlife Area, occupying the northern end of the lake of the same name, is the oldest bird sanctuary on the North American continent. More than 250 species of bird touch down here during their annual migrations south, including the spectacular whooping crane.

SASKATOON ★

Set on the banks of the South Saskatchewan River, Saskatoon is Saskatchewan's hip address. Home to a large university, and a world leader in agricultural biotechnology, the city also offers a host of outdoor activities and cultural events year-round, including a jazz festival, fringe and folk festivals, and the famous Shakespeare on the Saskatchewan theatre series. Once a major stop on the trans-Canadian rail network, the downtown area still has some impressive buildings from that era.

Saskatoon

University of Saskatchewan

College Dr.

Cumberland Ave.

GROSVENOR PARK

BRUNSKILL

Ewart Ave.

14th St. E.

ALBERT

Munroe Ave.

8th St. E.

Diefenbaker Canada Centre

River

Clarence Ave.

Mendel Art Gallery

Wanuskewin Heritage Park

Albert Ave.

Landsdowne Ave.

Kinsmen Park

Cres. East

University Bridge

Cosmopolitan Park

11th St. E.

University Dr.

Saskatchewan

Broadway Ave.

Ukrainian Museum of Canada

5th Ave. N.

Riverside Park

Spadina

Queen St.

4th Ave. N.

25th St. E.

CENTRAL BUSINESS DISTRICT

4th Ave. S.

Broadway Bridge

NUTANA

3rd Ave. N.

Hotel Senator

Bessborough

Victoria Ave.

2nd Ave. N.

22nd St. E.

3rd Ave. S.

21st St. E.

2nd Ave. S.

20th St. E.

Traffic Bridge

1st Ave. N.

CENTRAL INDUSTRIAL

23rd St. E.

1st Ave. S.

19th St. E.

Meewasin Valley Authority

Main St.

8th St. E.

Ontario Ave.

Pacific Ave.

Senator Sid Buckwold Bridge

Idylwyld Dr. N.

Idylwyld Dr. S.

Avenue B North

Avenue B South

Avenue C North

Avenue C South

RIVERSDALE

South

Avenue E North

Avenue E South

17th St. W.

Victoria Park

Avenue H North

Avenue H South

29th St. W.

WESTMOUNT

Avenue J North

Avenue J South

23rd St. W.

22nd St. W.

21st St. W.

19th St. W.

Avenue M North

Avenue M South

16th St. W.

SOUTH WEST INDUSTRIAL

13th St. W.

12th St. W.

11th St. W.

Scott Park

Leif Erickson Park

20th St. W.

Avenue P South

© ULYSSE/ULYSSES

▲   Saskatoon, Saskatchewan's largest city. © *Tourism Saskatchewan, F:11 Photographic Design*

Among the city's most striking buildings is the castle-like railway hotel, the **Bessborough**, which was built by relief workers during the depression era, as were the graceful arched bridges that span the river from downtown.

The **Mendel Art Gallery ★★★** is the province's best art museum. Its exhibits rotate quite regularly, and whether drawn from the permanent collection or just on loan, they're always interesting. Its eclectic collection means visitors can admire paintings by Canadian artist Emily Carr in one gallery, several different multimedia installations occupying another and a collection of modern prints, paintings and other media works by First Nations artists sprinkled throughout. The museum also contains such amenities as a children's room, a coffee shop and a gift shop.

A 10min drive north leads to the wonderful **Wanuskewin Heritage Park ★★★**, perhaps the best native museum in the prairies. The area around Saskatoon was settled continuously for thousands of years before the first white settlers arrived; a river valley just north of the city was long used as a "buffalo jump" where local First Nations hunted and established winter camps. Now the property is open to the public as a series of archaeological sites—ancient tipi rings and a medicine wheel, for instance—plus an indoor museum and interpretive centre dealing with the history of First Nations people here.

Saskatoon

▲ Wanuskewin Heritage Park at twilight.
© *Tourism Saskatchewan, Douglas E. Walker*

▲ An Aboriginal man in Wanuskewin Heritage Park. © *Tourism Saskatchewan, Douglas E. Walker*

YELLOWHEAD HIGHWAY

Veregin

Approximately 50km north off the Yellowhead Highway, Veregin houses the **National Doukhobour Heritage Village ★★**, an 11-building complex that throws light on one of the province's most intriguing immigrant groups. The Doukhobours came to Saskatchewan in 1899 and established a short-lived community here, eschewing meat, alcohol and tobacco in favour of an agrarian existence. They soon moved farther west, but this museum preserves the original prayer home and

machinery shop. Also on display are a brick oven, bath house, agricultural equipment and blacksmith's shop.

WEST CENTRAL AND NORTHERN SASKATCHEWAN

Around Duck Lake

Southwest of Prince Albert, Duck Lake was the site of one of the most famous events in Saskatchewan history: the battle between Louis Riel and his band of Metis and the North West Mounted Police. The **Duck Lake Regional Interpretive Centre ★★** describes the events as they unfolded, displaying artifacts from the Metis Resistance campaign. A series of painted outdoor murals welcome visitors, who can also climb a tower which provides a view of the battlefield grounds.

Located some 25km west of Duck Lake, **Fort Carlton Provincial Historic Park ★★** dates from 1810 and is another in the string of Hudson's Bay

LOUIS RIEL

Louis Riel and the Metis, descendants of French voya-
geurs and Aboriginal
people, made a signifi-
cant mark on prairie
history here in the
hills and valleys of
Saskatchewan. In
1884, after fighting
for the rights of the
Metis and being exiled
to the United States,
Riel was summoned by
the settlers of present-
day Saskatchewan, which at
the time was part of the vast
Northwest Territories. Riel's small
band, fighting for provincial status for
Saskatchewan and better treatment

▲ Louis Riel's funerary medallion.
© Philippe Renault

of Aboriginals and Metis, defeated Dominion troops in several early
skirmishes. But Riel never wanted a military conflict; rather, he hoped
for negotiation.

The Canadians, led by General James Middleton, waited for the victory
that seemed inevitable, since they outnumbered Riel's force—especially since a new coast-to-coast railroad was now capable of bringing
reinforcements quickly. The Metis were finally defeated at Batoche
in the last armed conflict on Canadian soil, and Riel was hanged as
a traitor; he is still a hero in some quarters of the province because
of his unwavering determination to retain his people's sovereignty.
Saskatchewan finally joined the Canadian Confederation in 1905.

Today, Riel's efforts have been recognized with the renaming of
Highway 11, which leads from Regina to Prince Albert via Saskatoon,
"The Louis Riel Trail."

Company posts in Saskatchewan. An important land treaty was also signed here. Today the site consists of a reconstructed stockade and buildings; a Visitor Centre with displays and interpretive trails explain how the fort was a Mountie post until the Battle of Duck Lake. Just outside the fort, a Plains Cree encampment—three tipis furnished in typical late-19th-century fashion—give a sense of what and how the natives traded with the English. The objects in these tipis include robes, skins, pipes, weapons and other ceremonial objects.

The park is most famous for wise old Archibald Bellaney, an Englishman who came here in 1931, took the name of Grey Owl, and lived on a remote lake. **Grey Owl's Cabin** ★, the one-room log cabin on Ajawaan Lake where Bellaney lived as a hermit for seven years, can only be reached by boat, canoe or—during summer—on foot via a 20km trail.

Batoche

Batoche National Historic Park ★ ★ ★ is where Riel's story came to its end in March of 1885. The site, a peaceful agricultural valley where the Metis had settled after moving westwards, became the capital of Metis resistance when Riel challenged the Canadian government. Today, a walking path, museum and interpretive staff guide visitors through the remains of the village of Batoche, including the restored St. Antoine de Padoue church and rectory. There are also trenches and rifle pits used by the Mountie forces during their four-day siege of Batoche.

Prince Albert National Park ★ ★ ★

Prince Albert National Park, encompassing 400,000ha, is one of Saskatchewan's finest parks. Entering from the south entrance on Route 263, visitors get to pass through grassland and fields, then aspen parklands and finally forests.

West Central and Northern Saskatchewan

Lac La Ronge Provincial Park ★ ★ ★

Lac La Ronge Provincial Park lies just north-east of Prince Albert Park on Route 2, providing similar scenery—and more of it, as this is the province's largest provincial park—than its better-known neighbour. There are more than 100 lakes here, including enormous Lac La Ronge, dotted with 1,305 islands. Cliffs, rock paintings and sand beaches can also be found in the park, and camping is available.

Lac La Ronge Park also contains one of the province's showcase historic sites, the **Holy Trinity Anglican Church Historic Site ★ ★ ★**—Saskatchewan's oldest standing building, an enormous structure in an oddly remote location. Built in the late 1850s from local wood,

▼ Prince Albert National Park, one of the most beautiful parks in the province.
© Tourism Saskatchewan, Douglas E. Walker

West Central and Northern Saskatchewan

▲ Holy Trinity Anglican Church.
© Saskatchewan Environment

▲ A few of the countless islands of Lac La Ronge. © Tourism Saskatchewan, Douglas E. Walker

then completed with stained-glass windows shipped from England, the church was part of the historic Stanley Mission.

Cumberland House Provincial Historic Park ★ ★ ★

Cumberland House Provincial Historic Park, on an island in the North Saskatchewan River near the Manitoba border, was quite important historically: it was the first Hudson's Bay Company fur post in western Canada. Later, it served as a port for steamboat traffic along the river. An 1890s-era powder house and part of a sternwheeler paddleboat are all that remain, but it's still a fascinating stop.

▶ One of the nearly 100 lakes of Lac La Ronge Provincial Park.
© Tourism Saskatchewan, Douglas E. Walker

Page 218

▶ A moonlit horseback ride.
© Tourism Saskatchewan, Douglas E. Walker

Manitoba

In the beginning, the province of Manitoba was occupied by several Aboriginal groups. It was they who gave the province its name: Manitou was a highly revered spirit among the First Nations who lived there, and the rapids of Lake Manitoba were believed to be his voice. Once the English and French arrived, however, the story of Manitoba swiftly became the story of a running feud between two rival fur-trading companies: the English-owned Hudson's Bay Company on the one hand and the French-Indian North West Company—which emerged later and, for a time, successfully competed against the British—on the other. This French influence is still evident today, most notably in Saint-Boniface.

The Metis made up a considerable part of this French-speaking population. The descendants of French trappers and Aboriginal people, the French-speaking, Catholic Metis lived at the forks of the Red and Assiniboine Rivers, in settlements which were annexed to Canada in 1869. Fearing for their language, education, land and religious rights, they were led by Louis Riel in their pursuit

of responsible government for the territory. What little they had was slowly being taken away, leading them to set up their own provisional government. The outrage over the trial and execution of Ontarian Orangeman Thomas Scott for defying the authority of this government forced Riel into exile in the United States. He did return to Canada, to Saskatchewan this time, to continue his fight and lead the Northwest Rebellion. Riel, the man who might have been the first premier of Manitoba, was executed for "treason" in 1885 and has been seen as a martyr by many ever since.

▼ Flax, a major Manitoba crop, with its blue flowers. © iStockphoto.com / Jostein Hauge

Manitoba

Churchill

Thompson

Snow Lake

Flin Flon

Grass River Prov. Park

39

10

Clearwater Lake Prov. Park

6

The Pas

Moose Lake

Cedar Lake

Grand Rapids

10

60

Lake Winnipegosis

Lake Winnipeg

Mafeking

Porcupine Prov. Forest

Birch River

Bowsman

6

Duck Mtn. Prov. Forest

10

Hecla/Grindstone Provincial Park

Manigotagan

Atikaki Provincial Wilderness Park

11

Nopiming Prov. Park

Roblin

5

Dauphin

5

Hodgson

Ashern

Riverton

Arborg

Lake Winnipeg

Inglis

Riding Mountain National Park

Eriksdale

7   8

17

Gimli

Grand Beach Prov. Park

St.Georges

Grand Marais

Whiteshell Provincial Park

Shellmouth

Wasagaming

5

Lake Manitoba

Winnipeg Beach Provincial Park

9

Selkirk

Beausejour

16

Neepawa

16

50

Oak Hammock Marsh

6

Lockport

Birds Hill Prov. Park

Minnedosa

Portage la Prairie

1

34

Austin

St François Xavier

2

⊛

Winnipeg

Dugald

Brandon

1

10

5

★ *Spruce Woods Prov. Park*

2

St.Norbert Prov. Park

Steinbach

3

75

12

Souris

23

Mariapolis

Morden

23

59

12

2

Glenora

3

14

Rosenfeld

Tolstoi

5

3

Pilot Mound

Winkler

3

Turtle Mtn. Prov. Park

3

Laugton

MINNESOTA (UNITED STATES)

NORTH DAKOTA (UNITED STATES)

SASKATCHEWAN

ONTARIO

©ULYSSE / ULYSSES

WINNIPEG ★★

The city was settled by a Scotsman named Thomas Douglas, fifth Earl of Selkirk, as a 187,000km² settlement called the Red River Colony (a monument at the end of Alexander Avenue marks the exact spot). Douglas was an emissary of the Hudson's Bay Company, and his responsibilities involved dividing up river lots—long, narrow parcels of land along the Red River.

The province's parliamentary business is taken care of in the **Manitoba Legislative Building ★★★**. This impressive property, is full of interesting touches like limestone walls embedded with fossils, two bronze bisons and a bust of Cartier. Up top, the dome is

capped with the 5.25m-tall **Golden Boy** ★★, a French sculpture of a boy covered in gold leaf carrying a sheaf of wheat underneath one arm and extending a torch toward the sky with the other.

Surrounding *The Leg* are landscaped gardens containing a fountain and a statue of Louis Riel. The original and more controversial sculpture of this Metis leader now stands across the river, at the eastern entrance to the Collège de Saint-Boniface.

The **Exchange District** ★★★, close to downtown, northwest of Portage and Main, is Winnipeg's former warehouse district—though today the stylish industrial buildings are home to new

▼ Winnipeg, capital of Manitoba. © *Philippe Renault*

Winnipeg

Archibald St.

La Seine

30

Provencher Blvd.

SAINT-BONIFACE

Higgins Ave.

Red River

Centre culturel franco-manitobain

Cathédrale Ave.

Maison Gabrielle-Roy ★

des Meurons St.

Av. Hamel

Saint-Jean-Baptiste St.

Marion St.

Langevin St.

St-Joseph St.

Cathédrale de Saint-Boniface ★

Louis Riel's Grave ★

Collège de Saint-Boniface ★

Musée de Saint-Boniface ★

Taché Ave.

115

1

St.Mary's Rd.

Lyndale Dr.

The Forks

Manitoba Children's Museum

1

Red River

River Ave.

Costume Museum of Canada ★

Manitoba Museum ★

Waterfront Dr.

52

Alexander Ave.

Main St.

Manitoba Centennial Centre

Lombard Ave.

52

Main St.

Garry St.

Smith St.

Assiniboine Ave.

Exchange District

Ross Ave.

City Hall

Arthur St.

85

Donald St.

Hargrave St.

Kennedy St.

Riel House National Historic Site ★

62

Osborne St.

Elgin Ave.

William St.

Bannatyne Ave.

McDermot Ave.

Notre Dame Ave.

Princess St.

Portage Ave.

Graham Ave.

St.Mary

York

Broadway

Kennedy St.

Manitoba Legislative Building ★

River

Cordova Ave.

62

Isabel St.

Cumberland Ave.

Carlton

Edmonton St.

Kennedy St.

Vaughan St.

Memorial

Blvd.

Colony

Broadway

Spence St.

Young St.

Winnipeg Art Gallery ★

Assiniboine

Furby St.

70

70

Sherbrook St.

62

70

67

Sargent Ave.

Maryland St.

Ave.

1

Chestnut St.

Toronto St.

Beverly St.

Home St.

St.Matthews Ave.

85

Wolseley

Westminster

70

Wellington Ave.

Arlington St.

Banning St.

Ingersoll St.

1

Academy Rd.

Garfield St.

Wolseley

Ave.

Wellington

Cr.

Wall St.

Erin St.

Assiniboine Park ★

Spruce St.

© ULYSSE / ULYSSES

occupants, such as antique shops, bookstores, theatre companies and the like. The federal government designated the area a National Historic Site in 1997.

The city's finest museums can be found near the Exchange District. Located within a complex of science attractions in the same downtown building, the **Manitoba Museum** ★ ★ ★ is Winnipeg's showcase museum, a tour de force emphasizing Manitoba's natural and social history. Separate galleries teach the visitor about the province's geology, grasslands ecology, Arctic ecology—a polar bear diorama is the star here—and Aboriginal history thanks to collections provided by the Hudson's Bay Company.

Nearby is the **Costume Museum of Canada** ★, which boasts a collection of 35,000 costumes, including some dating back 400 years and everything from Victorian gowns to 1970s swimsuits and linen tablecloths that belonged to Elizabeth I of England.

▶ The Manitoba Legislative Building with its *Golden Boy*. © iStockphoto.com / Leif Norman

▼ The unique architecture of Winnipeg's Exchange District. © iStockphoto.com / Deborah Clague

Housed in a striking triangular pale limestone building, the **Winnipeg Art Gallery** ★ ★ ★ is best known for its vast collection of Inuit art and sculptures. Founded in 1912, the museum boasts everything from 16th-century Flemish

▲ The Cathédrale de Saint-Boniface with its old facade in the foreground. © *Philippe Renault*

tapestry to modern art, and has a particularly strong collection of works by Canadian artists, decorative porcelains and silver.

Just across the Red River in the French-speaking neighbourhood of **Saint-Boniface**, the distinctive ruins of the **Cathédrale de Saint-Boniface ★★** are a must-see. The walls are all that remain of the church, which burned in 1968, but they are still very impressive. This was actually the fourth cathedral to stand on this spot. No wonder it remains a kind of shrine for Canada's largest French-speaking population outside of Québec.

In the cathedral's cemetery, **Louis Riel's grave** is marked by a simple red stone that belies the renown of the man who lies beneath it. Other stones on the lawn mark the graves of French settlers and Metis, including Chief One Arrow. There's also a glorious view of the river and the city skyline from this vantage point.

Behind the cathedral stands the silver-domed **Collège de Saint-Boniface**, established in the 1800s. A controversial sculpture of Louis Riel stands at its eastern entrance.

Winnipeg

Next door to the cathedral, the **Musée de Saint-Boniface** ★★ was built as a convent in 1846 and tells a number of fascinating stories about the city's French heritage; it is the oldest building in Winnipeg and one of the largest log structures in North America. The museum's exhibits delve into the lives of the region's French Canadians and Metis, but the star attraction here is the vast collection of items related to Louis Riel. Also notable is the tale it tells of the Grey Nuns (*Sœurs Grises*) who founded their convent after having travelled some 2,400km by canoe from Montréal.

Fans of writer Gabrielle Roy can see the house in which she grew up and where several of her works, including one of her most famous novels, *Street of Riches* (*Rue Deschambault*), are set. The **Maison Gabrielle-Roy** ★★ offers a unique glimpse into the life of this famous French-Canadian author. The house's ground floor has been magnificently restored with period furnishings, while the upper floors provide an overview of the author's life. You can visit the small attic where the young writer's imagination first took flight as she contemplated the view from her window.

GREATER WINNIPEG ★★

Assiniboine Park ★★ is a popular walking and cycling destination. The park's **English Gardens** ★★ are a wonderful surprise when in bloom: colourful carpets of daisies, marigolds, begonias, and more, artfully arranged beneath dark, shaggy columns of spruce trees.

▸ The Assiniboine Park Pavilion, a graceful historic building. © iStockphoto.com / Leif Norman

The park's most popular feature is the **Assiniboine Park Zoo** ★★★. More than 4,000 animals live here, including Russian lynx, a polar bear, kangaroos, snowy and great horned owls—even exotic residents like the South American vicuña and Siberian tigers. A statue of Winnie the Bear honours the famous Pooh's origins as a bear cub purchased by a Winnipeg soldier in Ontario and carried to England, where author A.A. Milne saw it and brought its story to a worldwide audience of children.

The **Riel House National Historic Site** ★★ paints a vivid picture of what life was like for the Metis in the Red

A FEW MANITOBA FESTIVALS

Folklorama, Winnipeg's huge annual summer bash is held during the first two weeks of August and covers a lot of ground: representatives of the city's many cultures—French, Ukrainian, Hungarian, Chinese, Japanese and East Indian, to name but a few—cook the food, sing the songs and dance the dances of their homelands in the many pavilions that spring up around the city for this event.

The **Winnipeg Fringe Theatre Festival** is one of the largest theatre festivals of its kind, featuring a mix of local talent and international groups who perform in various small downtown venues. Real discoveries can be made among the wide variety of shows, which range from family entertainment to experimental works. Free performances are held at Old Market Square throughout the festival.

Some 50,000 music lovers converge on Birds Hill Provincial Park for one fun-filled weekend each July to sing, dance, or simply enjoy the **Winnipeg Folk Festival**, one of North America's finest festivals of its kind.

The **Festival du Voyageur** is held in Saint-Boniface each February and celebrates winter and the fur trade era of the voyageurs who settled the province. Action at the big outdoor pavilion includes dog-sled races, snow sculptures and children's activities, while musical performers entertain the crowds at night.

During three days in early August, **Islendingadagurinn** (the Icelandic Festival of Manitoba) celebrates the local heritage from the far-off land of Iceland right in downtown Gimli. The festival includes a parade, music, poetry, Icelandic food and more.

The **Manitoba Sunflower Festival** celebrates the tall yellow flower for three days each July in Altona with Mennonite dancing, food and parades.

The **Manitoba Stampede and Exhibition** turns Morris, an otherwise sleepy town, into rodeo central for five days in mid-July. Surpassed only by the massive Calgary Stampede, it is Canada's second-largest rodeo.

The hugely popular **National Ukrainian Festival** takes place in Dauphin for three days in July or August, beginning on a Friday morning. Heritage village festivities include a bread-baking competition, embroidery contests, an Easter egg decorating competition, folk arts and lots of dancing.

The **Northern Manitoba Trappers' Festival** in The Pas runs for five days each February. Festivities here include a famous dog-sled race.

▼ A participant in Folklorama. © *Folklorama - Canada's Cultural Celebration / Andrew Sikorsky*

▲ Riel House. © *Parks Canada / Cornellier, A.*

his descendants until 1969. Riel's body lay in state here after he was executed for treason in December 1885.

EASTERN MANITOBA ★

Atikaki Provincial Wilderness Park ★ ★ ★

River Settlement. The tiny **Riel House** is set on a narrow river lot along the Red River. This building was home to famous Metis leader Louis Riel and his family for several years, and belonged to

Atikaki Provincial Wilderness Park, along the Ontario border, consists of a hodgepodge of cliffs, rock formations, pristine lakes and cascading rivers that spread over nearly 4,000km^2. It is extremely difficult to get to, however, requiring a canoe, a seaplane or several days of hiking to reach its interior; as a result, it contains the most unspoiled wilderness in the province's major parklands. Among the highlights are a series of rock murals painted by Aboriginals and a 20m waterfall well suited for

LA VÉRENDRYE (1685-1749)

Born in Trois-Rivières, Pierre Gaultier de Varennes entered the Seminary of Québec in 1696 and was initiated into the life of a soldier. Upon the death of his brother Louis, like him a second lieutenant in the Régiment de Bretagne, he took his nickname: La Vérendrye. In 1712, he married Marie-Anne Dandonneau du Sablé, with whom he would have six children.

A nomadic life had long beckoned, and in 1727 La Vérendrye joined the fur trading company founded by his brother Jacques-René on Lake Superior. After two years with the company, he concluded that exploring Lake Ouinipigon (Lake Winnipeg) and the "great Western river" (the Missouri River) would ultimately lead to the discovery of the Western Ocean (the Pacific Ocean).

La Vérendrye thus decided to form a company with several Montréal merchants. Accompanied by three of his sons (Jean-Baptiste, François

whitewater canoeing. Atikaki means "country of the caribou," and moose and caribou sightings are common.

Whiteshell Provincial Park ★ ★ ★

Further south, Whiteshell Provincial Park is Manitoba's largest and most beautiful park. Occupying some 2,720km², it is rich in lakes, rapids, waterfalls, fish and birds. There's something for everyone here: **Alf Hole Goose Sanctuary** ★ is among the best places in the province to see Canada geese, especially during migration; the rocks at **Bannock Point** ★, laid out by local First Nations to resemble the forms of snakes, fish, turtles and birds, are of archaeological interest; and the cliffs of **Lily Pond** ★, in Caddy Lake, are 3.75 billion years old.

Selkirk

On Route 9, Selkirk, a small river town marked by a giant catfish, is home to several important attractions. **Lower Fort Garry National Historic Site** ★ ★, just south of town, is a reconstitution of a trading post and pioneer village. It recalls the former importance of this post, which was built to replace the original Fort Garry in Winnipeg after it was carried away by flood waters.

Around Lake Winnipeg ★ ★

Winnipeg Beach Provincial Park has long been a favourite summer getaway for Winnipeg residents. Besides a well-known beach and boardwalk, the park's grounds also include a marina, a campground and a bay that's a favourite with windsurfers.

and Pierre), as well as some 50 volunteers, La Vérendrye left Montréal for the West in 1731, setting up trading posts along the way. During the journey, La Vérendrye's son Jean-Baptiste was killed by the Sioux. In 1738, La Vérendrye, accompanied by his son Louis-Joseph who had joined him and a group of men, finally cleared a route to the southwest via the Missouri River to reach the Western Ocean: the effort was in vain, though, because the Missouri, the "great Western river," led instead to the Gulf of Mexico via the Mississippi. He would go no further.

His son Pierre headed north in the spring of 1742, with the idea of building forts. For their part, Louis-Joseph and François refused to give up their idea of walking until they reached the Western Ocean. At the beginning of 1743, a giant wall of rock prevented them from going further. Disappointed, the two brothers backtracked. What they did not know was that they were the first French Canadians to have seen and described the eastern face of the Rockies, even though they never laid eyes on the Pacific.

▲ Discovering Manitoba's roots at Lower Fort Garry National Historic Site. © *Parks Canada / Cornellier, A.*

◀ The vast inland sea of Lake Winnipeg is a perfect sailing spot. © *iStockphoto.com / Deborah Clague*

Grand Beach Provincial Park is the most popular beach in Manitoba, hands down. Situated 100km north of Winnipeg, it boasts lovely white sand and grassy 8m-high dunes that seem to have been lifted directly from Cape Cod.

SOUTHERN MANITOBA

Steinbach

Located southeast of Winnipeg, Steinbach is the largest town in the region and features the popular **Mennonite Heritage Village ★★**, a 17ha village laid out in the traditional Mennonite style. The buildings focus on the lives of the Mennonites, people of Dutch origin who started emigrating to the province from Russia in 1874.

Turtle Mountain Provincial Park ★ ★

Turtle Mountain Provincial Park, composed of compacted coal and glacial deposits, rises more than 250m above the surrounding prairie land. Explorer La Vérendrye called it the "blue jewel of the plains," and its gentle hills lend themselves to mountain biking, horseback riding and hiking. There is also, of course, a considerable population of the beautiful painted turtles that gave the mountain its name.

CENTRAL MANITOBA

Portage la Prairie

West of Winnipeg lies Portage la Prairie, founded in 1738 by French-Canadian explorer Pierre Gaultier de la Vérendrye as a resting stop on the canoe route to Lake Manitoba. The

Central Manitoba

FLIN FLON

Flin Flon is Canada's most whimsically named municipality and greets visitors with a jumble of streets climbing the rocky hills. Located mostly in Manitoba, with a smaller part spilling over into Saskatchewan, Flin Flon is the most important mining centre in this part of the country, and has grown to become the province's sixth-largest city.

Flin Flon was named by a group of gold prospectors in 1915 who found a copy of a mass-market science fiction paperback named *The Sunless City* during a northern Manitoba portage. Later, on a lakeshore near here, they staked a mining claim and named it for the book's main character, Josiah Flintabbatey Flonatin, or *Flinty* to locals. Thus, the green 7.5m-tall Josiah Flintabbatey Flonatin statue presides over the city's entrance. It was designed for the city by the renowned American cartoonist Al Capp.

town's most interesting natural attraction is the crescent-shaped lake (fittingly named Crescent Lake), a cutoff bow of the Assiniboine River that nearly encircles the entire downtown. **Island Park** ★ sits within that crescent, providing beautiful tree-shaded picnic spots by the water.

Spruce Woods Provincial Park ★ ★

The "Spirit Sands," a desert landscape of immense sand dunes in Spruce Woods Provincial Park, never fails to take visitors by surprise. Self-guided trails take hikers through the dunes and the surrounding spruce forests and prairie, and to the "Devil's Punch Bowl," an unusual pond created by underground streams.

Campgrounds and a sandy beach for swimming make this large park popular in the summer.

WESTERN MANITOBA

Riding Mountain National Park ★ ★ ★

Riding Mountain National Park rises majestically from the plains with aspen-covered slopes that are habitats for wild animals such as elk, moose, deer, wolves and lynx. The largest black bear ever seen in North America was killed here by a poacher in 1992, and bison are contained within a large bison enclosure near Lake Audy.

▶   Riding Mountain National Park.
     © *Parks Canada / Barrett & Mackay*

▲　Grain elevators, a symbol of Manitoba. © *Inglis Grain Elevators National Historic Site*

PRAIRIE CATHEDRALS

There used to be a grain elevator and a town every 16km along the railway line that follows Highway 61, and throughout the prairies for that matter. The old elevator system was established in the 1880s and based on the premise that a farmer and his horsedrawn carriage could only haul grain over about 16km in one day.

The advent of longhaul trucks put an end to the need for so many elevators and the phasing out of a government transportation subsidy forced the construction of a new generation of elevators. The more sophisticated "high throughputs" can hold more grain, handle the drying and cleaning and load the grain more quickly into the railcars.

As a result, grain elevators are being torn down so quickly that they will be extinct within the next 20 years, and maybe even sooner (some 6,000 grain elevators could be found in the Prairies during the 1930s; there are now less than 1,000). The Provincial Museum of Alberta has amassed a collection of old photographs to immortalize these cathedrals before they disappear forever.

In Inglis, Manitoba, a dedicated volunteer group has gone a step further, by restoring a row of grain elevators which has become a National Historic Site.

Route 19 begins in the centre of the park and travels a switchback path up (or down) the park's steepest ridge. The naturalist Grey Owl, an Englishman who passed himself off as an Aboriginal person, lived here for six months, giving talks with his two tamed beavers, Jerryroll and Rawhide (he spent most of his time in Prince Albert National Park, however); the remote **Grey Owl's Cabin** ★ is located 17km up a hiking trail off Route 19.

Inglis

As the "sentinels of the prairies" rapidly disappear from the landscape, the **Inglis Grain Elevators** ★ stand as a reminder of the golden era of the Canadian West. A row of five standard wooden grain elevators is being preserved as a National Historic Site, allowing visitors to see for themselves these impressive wooden structures.

NORTHERN MANITOBA ★

Churchill

There are no roads linking Churchill to the rest of the province; it can only be reached by train or airplane. Isolated and cold, Churchill nevertheless beguiles travellers with its remoteness and stunning wildlife. The place is important historically as well, as this is where the English first established a foothold in Manitoba. They chose the site because of a superb natural harbour, so it's fitting that the town's dominant fea-

▲ A view of Hudson Bay in Manitoba's far north. © iStockphoto.com / Trevor Bauer

▶ The polar bear, an excellent hunter of the far north. © iStockphoto.com / David T Gomez

▲   The one-of-a-kind York Factory National Historic Site. © *Parks Canada / Mercier, F.*

ture today is a huge grain elevator beside the docks.

The townsite is also located right in the middle of the migratory path of the area's polar bear population, which is a mixed blessing for the town's inhabitants. While these majestic animals attract visitors from around the world to this remote spot every autumn, they also wander right into town occasionally, posing a potential risk to anyone who crosses their path. In addition to the bears, people also come here. They come to see caribou, seals, birds and especially white beluga whales in summer. And there is always the possibility of an astonishing display of the aurora borealis, or northern lights.

The city's **Eskimo Museum** ★★★ maintains one of the world's pre-eminent collections of Inuit artifacts. Founded in 1944 by the local Roman Catholic Diocese, it contains artifacts dating from as far back as 1700BC. A set of ornately carved walrus tusks is among its most impressive pieces.

The **York Factory National Historic Site** ★★★, 250km southeast of Churchill, is what remains of the Hudson Bay Company fur-trade post that first established the English in western Canada. A wooden depot built in 1832 still stands here, and there are ruins of a stone gunpowder magazine and a cemetery with markers dating back to the 1700s.

Major Themes

Seasons

The climate of Western Canada varies widely from one region to another. The Vancouver area benefits from a sort of micro-climate thanks to its geographic location between the Pacific and the mountains. Temperatures in Vancouver vary between 0°C and 15°C in the winter and much warmer in the summer.

The high altitudes of the Rocky Mountains and the winds of the Prairies make for a varied climate throughout the rest of the region. Winters are cold and dry and temperatures can drop to –40°C, though the average is about –20°C. Winnipeg and Saskatoon are the coldest cities in Canada in winter. Winters in southern Alberta are often marked by the phenomenal Chinook wind which can melt several feet of snow is a matter of hours. Summers are dry, with temperatures staying steady around 25°C on the plains and lower in the mountains.

WINTER

December to March is the ideal season for winter-sports enthusiasts (skiing, skating, etc.). Warm clothing is essential during this season (coat, scarf, hat, gloves, wool sweaters and boots). On the other hand, Vancouver has a particularly wet winter, so visitors should pack a raincoat. In southern British Columbia the mercury rarely falls below 0.

▲ Fine travelling weather! © VIA Rail

▶ A dogsled excursion.
© Tourism Saskatchewan, Douglas E. Walker

Seasons

▲ The myriad colours of autumn.
© *Tourism Saskatchewan, Douglas E. Walker*

SPRING AND FALL

Spring is short (end of March to end of May) and is characterized by a general thaw leading to wet and muddy conditions. Fall is often cool. A sweater, scarf, gloves, windbreaker and umbrella will therefore come in handy.

SUMMER

Summer lasts from the end of May to the end of August. Visitors should bring along t-shirts, lightweight shirts and pants, shorts and sunglasses; a sweater or light jacket is a good idea for evenings. Hikers should remember that temperatures are cooler at higher altitudes.

▲ The Bow River snakes through the Rockies.
© *iStockphoto.com / Arpad Benedek*

Next pages

▶ Canoeing on the historic Churchill River.
© *iStockphoto.com / Jason Verschoor*

Seasons

Summer Activities

HIKING

Accessible to most everyone, hiking is an activity that can be enjoyed in all national and most provincial parks. Before setting out, you should plan your excursion well by checking the length and level of difficulty of each trail.

Some parks have long trails that require more than a day of hiking and lead deep into the wild. When taking one of these trails, which can stretch dozens of kilometres, it is crucial to respect all signs. There are maps that show the trails and the locations of wilderness campsites and shelters.

To make the most of an excursion, it is important to bring along the right equipment. You'll need a good pair of walking shoes, appropriate maps, sufficient food and water and a small first-aid kit containing a pocket knife and bandages.

BICYCLING

Visitors can go bicycling and mountain biking all over Western Canada, along the usually quiet secondary roads or the trails crisscrossing the parks. The roads offer prudent cyclists one of the most enjoyable means possible to tour these picturesque regions. Keep in mind, however, that distances in these vast provinces can be very long.

Mountain biking trails have been created in a number of parks. The parks' information centre can provide information about these.

◄ Finding serenity, tranquility, and peace…
© *Travel Alberta*

▲   Escaping the big city with an outing in Vancouver's Stanley Park. © *iStockphoto.com / Zennie*

Many bike shops offer a rental service. Sufficient insurance is a good idea when renting a bicycle. Some places include insurance against theft in the cost of the rental.

CANOEING

Many parks are strewn with lakes and rivers which canoe-trippers can spend a day or more exploring. Wilderness campsites have been laid out to accommodate canoers during long excursions. Canoe rentals and maps of possible routes are usually available at the parks' information centres. It is always best to have a map that indicates the length of the portages in order to determine how physically demanding the trip will be. Carrying a canoe, baggage and food on your back is not always a pleasant experience. A 1km portage is generally considered long, and will be more or less difficult depending on the terrain.

BEACHES

Whether you decide to stretch out on the white sand of Long Beach on Vancouver Island, or prefer the more family-oriented atmosphere of Qualicum Beach, with its calm waters, or Wreck Beach, the driftwood-carvers' rendez-vous, you'll discover one of Western Canada's most precious natural attractions, British Columbia's Pacific Coast. Swimming is not always possible, however, because of the heavy surf and cold water temperatures of the North Pacific.

Summer Activities

Summer Activities

FISHING

In Western Canada, anglers can cast their line in the ocean or in one of the many rivers and lakes. Don't forget, however, that fishing is a regulated activity. Fishing laws are complicated, so it is wise to request information from the four provinces ahead of time and obtain the brochure stating key fishing regulations. Furthermore, keep in mind that there are different permits for fresh water and salt water fishing. Most permits or licenses can be purchased at major sporting-goods stores.

As a general rule, however, keep in mind that:

• it is necessary to obtain a permit from a provincial government before going fishing;

• a special permit is usually required for salmon fishing;

• fishing seasons, which vary depending on the species, are established by the appropriate ministry and must be respected at all times;

• fishing is permitted in national parks, but you must obtain a permit from park officials beforehand.

▲   A beautiful fishing spot.
© *Tourism Saskatchewan, Douglas E. Walker*

GOLF

Magnificent golf courses, renowned for their remarkable natural settings, can be found throughout Western Canada. Stretching along the ocean, or through narrow mountain valleys, these courses boast exceptional views and challenging holes. A few courses

THE TRANS CANADA TRAIL

The Trans Canada Trail, a fascinating multi-purpose trail, was inaugurated on September 9, 2000. Once completed, it will be the longest trail of its kind in the world, covering some 16,000km from one end of Canada to the other. It will connect St. John's, the capital of Newfoundland and Labrador, to Victoria, the capital of British Columbia, and will include a northern portion starting in the Alberta city of Calgary and leading to Tuktoyaktuk in the Northwest Territories and Chesterfield Inlet in Nunavut. The trail will be used for walking, hiking, cross-country skiing, cycling, horseback riding and snowmobiling, and will include both existing trails and new segments. The project is financed through public donations and government subsidies, and almost 10,000km of trail have already been marked to date. For more information, visit the Trans Canada Trail's Web site at **www. tctrail.ca**.

have been laid out in provincial parks (in Kananaskis Country) and near the parks of the Rockies (in the Columbia River Valley), where peace and quiet reign supreme and luxurious hotels are just a short distance away.

WHALE-WATCHING

Whales are common along the coasts of British Columbia. Visitors wishing to catch a closer view of these impressive but harmless sea mammals can take part in a whale-watching cruise or go sea-kayaking. The most commonly sighted species are orcas (also known as killer whales), humpbacks, which head to the waters off the coast of Mexico in spring, and grey whales. These excursions usually start from the northeastern end of Vancouver Island, in Johnstone Strait, or from Long Beach, on the southwestern end.

SEAL-WATCHING

Seals are also found along British Columbia's coasts, and anyone wishing to observe them from close up can take part in an excursion designed for that purpose. Occasionally, attracted by the boat, these curious mammals will pop their heads out of the water right nearby, and gaze, with their big, black eyes, at the passengers.

▼ Seals basking in the sunshine.
  © Pierre Longnus

BIRDWATCHING

The wilds of Western Canada attract all sorts of birds, which can easily be observed with the help of binoculars. Some of the more noteworthy species that you might spot are hummingbirds, golden eagles, bald eagles, peregrine falcons, double-crested cormorants,

▲ A Saskatchewan golf course in a beautiful
    natural setting.
    © *Tourism Saskatchewan, Douglas E. Walker*

▶ Birdwatching in the half-light of evening.
    © *Tourism Saskatchewan, Douglas E. Walker*

pelicans, grouse, ptarmigans, countless varieties of waterfowl including
the mallard, barnacle goose, Canada
goose, trumpeter swan (which migrates
from the Arctic to Mexico) and finally
the grey jay, a little bird who will gladly
help itself to your picnic lunch if you
aren't careful.

For help identifying them, purchase a
copy of the *Peterson Field Guide: A Field
Guide to Western Birds*, published by
Houghton Mifflin. Although parks are
often the best places to observe certain
species, bird-watching is an activity that
can be enjoyed anywhere.

Winter Activities

DOWNHILL SKIING

Known the world over for downhill skiing, the mountains of Western Canada attract numerous downhill skiers every year. The most popular ski hills are located around Banff and Jasper and north of Vancouver at Whistler and Blackcomb. Fans of powder skiing are whisked to the highest summits of the Rockies by helicopter, and deposited there to enjoy the ski of their lives.

CROSS-COUNTRY SKIING

Some parks, like those in Kananaskis Country and in the Rocky Mountains, are renowned for their long cross-country ski trails. Daily ski rentals are available at most ski centres.

SNOWBOARDING

Snowboarding appeared at the beginning of the 1990s. While a marginal activity at first, the sport quickly caught on, to the point that today's North American ski hills often have more snowboard-

ers than skiers. And no wonder! With snowboarding, the excitement of hitting the slopes is fivefold.

In spite of common perception, snowboarding is not just for the young; there is no age limit for enjoying the pleasures of a slalom run. For beginners, a few lessons are a good idea before heading out, and many ski hills offer this service. Most also rent equipment.

SNOWMOBILING

This winter activity has many fans in the West, where each province is crisscrossed by several kilometres of trails. For more information on the provincial trail system, clubs and events, contact the BC Snowmobile Federation, the Alberta Snowmobile Association, the Saskatchewan Snowmobile Association or the Snowmobilers of Manitoba Inc.

You can explore these four provinces by snowmobile, but be sure to respect regulations. Furthermore, don't forget

◀ A winter landscape with white-clad mountains. © iStockphoto.com / Philippe Widling

▶ A freestyle cross-country skier.
© Tourism Saskatchewan, Douglas E. Walker

that a permit is required and that it is also advisable to take out liability insurance.

The following rules should be respected at all times: stay on the snowmobile trails; always drive on the right side of the trail; wear a safety helmet; and keep the snowmobile's headlights on both day and night.

▲ A winter bonfire under the northern lights.
© *Tourism Saskatchewan, Douglas E. Walker*

◀ A snowboarder displays his skills.
© *Travel Alberta*

Flora

While the plains only cover a small part of British Columbia, 56% of the province's territory is covered by forest. The forest growing along the coast, Haida Gwaii (Queen Charlotte Islands) and on the west coast of Vancouver Island is so lush that it is called northern rain forest, the counterpart of the tropical rain forest. Douglas firs and western red cedars abound, as does the Sitka spruce. The Douglas fir can grow to up to 90m in height and 4.5m in diameter. This forest receives up to 4,000mm of rain per year and many of its trees are more than 1,000 years old, though most of the ancient Douglas firs were cut down in the last century. Much higher and drier, the province's interior is home to vast pine, spruce and hemlock forests.

Larches grow in the sub-alpine forests found at higher altitudes. The larch is the only coniferous tree in Canada that loses its needles in the fall, after they turn yellow. They grow back in the spring.

Sheltered by Vancouver Island, the southern Gulf Islands have a relatively dry, mild climate. You'll even find certain varieties of cacti here, including the prickly pear. Flowers bloom in this area all year round, especially in the months of April and May.

The prairies stretch from southeast Alberta to Ontario. Grasses cover the land, except along the rivers, where

▲ Giant pine cones. © *Travel Alberta*

▶ Dense temperate rainforest.
   © *Pierre Longnus*

cottonwood and willow trees grow. Cacti are also common in the southernmost areas. The prairies rise and become hilly as you head west into the foothills, where aspen, white spruce, lodgepole pine and Douglas fir trees grow.

A belt of aspen parkland acts as a transition zone between the grasslands of the south and the boreal forest of the north. Aspen parkland and grasslands cover most of this area. Beyond this, more than half the territory is covered with boreal forest dotted with lakes, bogs, and marshland. White spruce, lodgepole pine and balsam fir are the most common trees. Finally, parts of this region are strewn with bushes bearing raspberries and saskatoon berries.

▲　Seeing the forest for the trees. © Pierre Longnus

◀　Row on row of hay bales. © Pierre Longnus

◀　Narrow valleys carve their way through the fields. © Pierre Longnus

◀　Snow melts away under the sun. © Travel Alberta

RESPECT THE MOUNTAIN!

"Protection, conservation and enhancement" are the watchwords of the national parks. Because of the management costs that this rule entails, charges for services in national parks, such as camping, may be higher than those found in private organizations. But to help visitors better understand the importance of our natural heritage, interpretation activities are often offered free of charge. Ecotourism in national parks involves practising recreational and educational activities respectfully, which requires a thorough understanding of guidelines and socially responsible behaviour.

For more information, visit the **Parks Canada** Website (www.pc.gc.ca).

Here are a few guidelines:

- First of all, stay on the trails even if they are covered in snow or mud, in order to protect the ground vegetation and avoid widening the trail.

- Unless you're heading off on a long trek, wear lightweight hiking boots; they do less damage to vegetation.

- When in a group in alpine regions, spread out and walk on rocks as much as possible to avoid damaging the vegetation.

- It is just as important to protect waterways, bodies of water and the ground water when in mountainous regions. When digging back-country latrines, place them at least 30m from all water sources, and cover everything (tissue paper included) with earth.

- Never clean yourself in lakes or streams.

- At campsites, dispose of waste water only in designated areas.

- Never leave any garbage behind. Bags for this are provided at Parks Canada offices.

- Certain types of flowers are endangered, so do not pick anything.

- Leave everything as you find it, so those that follow can enjoy the beauty of nature as you did.

Fauna

Warmed by the Japanese current, the waters of the Pacific maintain a higher temperature than those of the Atlantic, which are cooled by the Labrador current. As a result, this region features very distinctive marine life. For example, this is the only place in Canada where sea otters are found, even though they were almost completely exterminated by hunting. Sea lions are also indigenous to the Pacific coast. Many animals feast on the abundant salmon on the coast and in the rivers where they spawn. Grizzly bears, for example, gather for a feast when the rivers are teeming with salmon, and gourmets that they are, eat only the roe and the head! Wolves, black bears, raccoons, gulls and bald eagles eat the leftovers. Speaking of bald eagles, the Pacific coast is home to Canada's largest population of these majestic birds, which have all but disappeared from the Atlantic coast.

Countless orcas inhabit the waters around Vancouver Island and are commonly spotted from the ferries that link this island with the mainland. They are the only marine mammals that eat warm-blooded animals like seals, belugas and other smaller whales, which probably explains their more common appellation, killer whales.

▼ An orca, the largest member of the dolphin family. © *Pierre Longnus*

▼ Seals resting. © *Tourism Powell River*

▼ The gliding flight of gulls. © *Pierre Longnus*

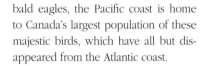

▲ A sharp-tailed grouse, the provincial bird of Saskatchewan. © *Tourism Saskatchewan*

▶ An adult deer and its fawn. © *Travel Alberta*

With the arrival of fall, certain marine mammals, like the grey whale, migrate from Alaska to Baja California in Mexico. They make their way back up to Alaska in the spring.

Large numbers of cougars inhabit British Columbia's forests, particularly on Vancouver Island, where they feed on Columbia blacktail deer.

An impressive variety of birds and mammals inhabit the Priaries. Some of the more noteworthy winged species are bald eagles found around the northern lakes, and prairie and peregrine falcons, which can often be seen in and around the plains either diving for prey or waiting patiently on a fence post by the highway. Finally, the migratory path of the trumpeter swan passes through Alberta.

To the delight of anglers, the lakes and rivers of Western Canada are teeming with countless freshwater fish, including eight different varieties of trout.

Fauna

BEARS

In their miniature stuffed form, bears were our childhood best friends, but in real life they are ferocious and fearsome carnivores. The grizzly and the black bear are the only bears in the Canadian Rockies. Because bears hibernate, their survival depends on accumulating enough fat stores to carry them through the winter. Thanks to their extremely keen sense of smell, bears can detect the presence of hikers before hikers can spot them. To avoid an unlucky meeting with a bear, make noise throughout your hike to signal your presence. Don't forget that a bear that approaches humans and seems docile is still a bear: unpredictable and able to attack without warning.

Black Bear

The black bear is the smallest bear in North America. As its name suggests, it is usually black, although there are some with dark brown fur. Its head is quite high and the line between its shoulders and its hindquarters is much straighter than on a grizzly. The male weighs between 170 and 200kg and can grow to up to 160cm in height. The black bear is found throughout most of North America. Its facial

▲ A grizzly bear. © *Travel Alberta*

profile (around the muzzle) is fairly straight, unlike the grizzly's, which is concave. In the Rockies, these bears are most often found in dense forests at lower altitudes and in the clearings of mixed conifer and broadleaf forests, usually near a lake or a river.

Grizzly Bear

Also known as the silvertip bear, the grizzly is a powerful carnivore of imposing size. The grizzly's colouring varies between brown and blond and its fur often appears to be greying, hence its name. Larger and heavier than its cousin the black bear, the grizzly measures up to 2m when standing on its hind legs. Its average weight is about 200kg. It is often difficult to tell a young grizzly from an adult black bear. You run the greatest risk of meeting a grizzly in the valleys and prairies of sub-alpine environments and in alpine tundra.

THE AMERICAN BISON

The American bison, the largest land mammal in North America, is divided into two subspecies: the plains bison and the wood buffalo. During the 19th century, 30 to 70 million plains bison roamed the great North American prairies, and Aboriginal peoples drew most of their subsistence from them: food, clothing and skins to cover their dwellings. At the same time, some 170,000 wood buffalo lived in the northern portions of what are now the provinces of Alberta and British Columbia and the Northwest Territories.

The wood buffalo is much larger than the plains bison; its forelegs are almost bare, and its forelock falls in long tufts over its forehead. The plains bison has a long mane that reaches below its chest, and its coat forms a thick tuft between its horns.

After the arrival of the Europeans, governments wanted to exterminate the bison because the species, along with the Aboriginal peoples it fed, was hampering the progress of civilization (most notably that of agriculture). They almost succeeded in attaining their goal: in 1895, there were fewer than 100 bison in the United States and around 300 in Canada, but there were still plenty of Aboriginals...

The country's national parks were eventually created to protect the surviving bison and allow them to reproduce. Elk Island National Park, located around 65km east of Edmonton, the capital of Alberta, is today home to some 600 plains bison and 350 wood buffalo. Wood Buffalo National Park, which stretches over northern Alberta and the southern Northwest Territories, is home to over 2,000 bison.

When the bison numbered in the millions, Aboriginals used various hunting techniques, including forcing the bison to throw themselves off a cliff and killing them through hunting with horses and guns. The Head-Smashed-In Buffalo Jump, located around 15kms northwest of Fort Macleod, Alberta, is one of the best preserved sites in North America where Aboriginals, along corridors flanked with rocky cairns they had created, forced bison to jump off a cliff not far from a vast pasture. This was before the arrival of the horse (and the European colonists).

Architecture

The sharp geographical contrast—it could even be called a clash—between British Columbia and the Prairies has led to the development of two very different styles of architecture—as is true of the other arts as well. The blanket of forests and mountains that covers two thirds of the Canadian West, combined with the coastal climate, which is much milder than in the rest of Canada, is juxtaposed with the bare Prairies, where the climatic conditions are among the harshest in Canada, and the deep snow is blown by violent winds during the long winter months.

The Aboriginal people were the first to adapt to these two extremes. Some developed a sedentary architecture with openings looking out onto the sea and the natural surroundings; others, a nomadic architecture designed primarily to keep out the cold and the wind. Thanks to the mild climate along the coast and the presence of various kinds of wood that were easy to carve, the Salish and the Haida were able to erect complex and sophisticated structures. Their totem poles, set up in front of long-houses made with the carefully squared trunks of red cedars, still stood along the beaches of the Queen Charlotte Islands near the end of the 19th century. These linear villages provided everyone with direct access to the ocean's resources.

On the other side of the Rocky Mountains, the Prairie peoples turned the hides of bison to good account, using them to make clothing, build homes and even to make shields with which to defend themselves. Their homes, commonly known as tipis,

▲   The reconstructed village of Ksan.
  © *Pierre Longnus*

◀   Tipis of the old plains. © *Glenbow Archives; NA-668-17*

Previous pages

◀   The pristine waters of a peaceful lake.
  © *iStockphoto.com / Vera Bogaerts*

could be easily taken down and packed up for transportation. They consisted of a thin cone-shaped structure made with the woody stems of shrubs and covered with hides sewn together with animal tendons.

The first Europeans to exploit the natural resources of the Canadian West took refuge in palisade forts that doubled as fur trading posts during peacetime. They erected these rectangular structures between the mountains and the plains during the first half of the 19th century to protect themselves from warlike Aboriginals. Some interesting reconstructions can be found in a number of places.

On the West Coast, peace and easy living provided a fertile environment for the introduction of Loyalist architecture from Upper Canada, as evidenced by Victoria's St. Ann's Schoolhouse (1858)—replaced in 1871 by St. Ann's Academy when the schoolhouse was deemed too small—and Wentworth Villa (1862). These structures are shingled and painted white, and have sash windows with small panes of glass. During the second half of the 19th century, this type of building quickly gave way to elaborate Victorian architecture, which made maximum use of the region's abundance of soft wood, which was easy to cut and turn mechanically.

With Canadian Pacific's construction of a transcontinental railroad and the opening of coal mines in Alberta and British Columbia, all sorts of new towns sprang up, each with its own destiny in store. During their first years of existence, all of them had boomtown architecture, characterized by rows of buildings with prefabricated wooden structures, often imported from eastern

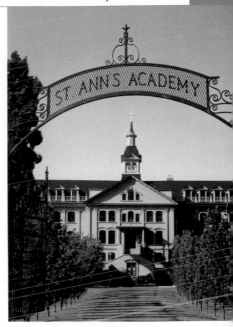

▲ St. Ann's Academy in Victoria.
© *Provincial Capital Commission*

Canada, and a false front that concealed a smaller interior. Some of these façades were adorned with a prominent cornice or a whimsically shaped parapet.

Upon completing its transcontinental railway in 1886, Canadian Pacific began building a nationwide network of luxury hotels and took particular interest in the Canadian West from the outset. It erected hotels and train stations in the Château style, which over the years became the company's trademark and the country's "national" style. The Banff Springs Hotel, erected in 1903, and the Empress Hotel in Victoria (1908), both graced with tall, sloping roofs and adorned with Renaissance details, at once reminiscent of the manors of Scotland and the châteaux of the Loire, are the finest examples.

At the beginning of the 20th century, British Columbia residents of English and Scottish extraction began develop-

Architecture

ing a taste for the temperate natural environment in which they were living, and also seem to have become infatuated with the first part of their province's name. Lovely landscaped gardens full of flowers that couldn't survive anywhere else in Canada became all the rage, particularly in Vancouver and Victoria. In the midst of these magnificent green spaces, huge Tudor Revival and Arts & Crafts houses were built. These two styles originated in the so-called "back to basics" movement led by British immigrants. The Tudor Revival style was inspired by the manors that were built in the English countryside under the reign of Henry VIII, and was characterized by the use of red-brick facing, bay windows with stone mullions and surbased gothic arches.

The Arts & Crafts movement, which could be described as both a craze for rural British crafts and a rejection of the industrialization of big cities, produced an organic architecture featuring extensions covered with different materials, ranging from half-timbering to walls made of stones from the beach. Everything was skilfully designed to produce an overall effect of great charm. Vancouver architects Maclure and Fox excelled in this domain, and a good example of this style is the Walter C. Nichol House (1402 The Crescent, Shaughnessy Heights, Vancouver).

The public buildings that were erected during the same period are more urban in style, as was required by their function. Here, too, however, the emphasis was on British styles and architects. Sir Francis Rattenbury, who designed Victoria's Legislature and Vancouver's former courthouse (now the Vancouver Art Gallery), was the leading light of this prosperous era.

The end of World War II marked the beginning of a new era of unprecedented prosperity throughout the region. Using wood, and then concrete, individuals like Robert Berwick, C.E. Pratt, Ron Thom and more recently Arthur Erickson designed buildings according to the elementary post and beam method, and erected them on the Coast Mountains. The pure lines of these structures blend into the luxuriant greenery that envelops the communal rooms, while the wall-to-wall picture windows that fill in the voids highlight the panoramas of the Pacific Ocean (Robert Berwick, Berwick House, 1560 Ottawa Avenue, Vancouver, 1939; Erickson and Massey, Gordon Smith house, The Byway, Vancouver, 1965). Until that

▲ Calgary, Alberta's booming metropolis. © *iStockphoto.com / Arpad Benedek*

time, only houses in the fishing ports of Vancouver Island had had any openings looking out onto the sea.

In Alberta, the prosperity of the 1970s and 1980s led to massive development in the cities of Edmonton and Calgary. Skyscrapers sprang up like mushrooms, changing both skylines considerably in just a decade. In Calgary, a network of skywalks known as the "+15" was put in place, so that office workers and shoppers could make their way from one building to another without facing the winter cold. In addition, the sprawling suburbs of the two rival cities gobbled up several kilometres of the surrounding countryside. Both places are steeped in mainstream North American culture, as evidenced so clearly by the enormous West Edmonton Mall, where the "teachings" of Disneyworld and Las Vegas blend together in a whirl of gaudy commercialism.

However, since 1985, individuals like Douglas Cardinal, an Aboriginal architect from Alberta, have been trying to develop a style more in harmony with the particularities of the Alberta plains. The undulating shapes of Douglas Cardinal's buildings, which look as if they have been sculpted by the violent winds that sweep the Prairies, have gained international recognition.

Architecture

Next pages
▸ The gorges and eternal snows of the Rockies.
© *VIA Rail*

First Nations

After coming within a hair's breadth of vanishing completely, due to the illnesses to which they were exposed through their contact with European settlers in the late 19th century, the First Nations of the West are now seeing a substantial growth in their population. In 1870, there were fewer than 80,000 Aboriginals in British Columbia. It has since climbed back up to more than 196,000 (2006), accounting for about 4.8% of the province's total population.

Though the Aboriginal population is growing considerably, it would be incorrect to speak of a real "renaissance," since a number of nations have vanished forever, taking their rites and traditions along with them. Other communities have become more visible, but their future is still uncertain.

Two thirds of western Aboriginals live on reserves. Some of these pieces of land are the size of Switzerland, while others aren't even as big as Manhattan. A notable case in point is the Capilano reserve in North Vancouver, which barely covers three blocks and is completely surrounded by the city. The reserves were created by the *Indian Act*, adopted in 1867 by the federal government of Canada, and do not always correspond to the traditional territory of the various nations.

Aboriginals living on reservations are entitled to certain privileges. They pay no income tax, nor any goods and ser-

vices taxes. They also have the right to free education from primary school through university. Finally, health-related expenses such as eye exams, glasses and dental care are paid by the state. Until the 1950s, the *Indian Act* also attempted to strip Aboriginal people of their traditional culture, by forbidding their languages, ceremonies and rituals. Children were separated from their families and sent to residential schools, where they were forced to learn and speak only English and to wear Western clothing, to the extent that when the families were reunited, the parents and the children could no longer understand each other.

Since 1960, the Aboriginals of British Columbia have been struggling to revive their culture and traditions. The Haida artists of the Queen Charlotte Islands have become known around the world for their carving, especially totem poles and jewellery.

The only treaty signed in British Columbia in modern times came into effect in 2000, and not without controversy. The Nisga'a Nation was awarded 2,000km^2 of land in the lower Nass Valley, in northern British Columbia, subsurface rights and powers of self-government. In 2002, the Haida Nation initiated a lawsuit in which they claim title to Haida Gwaii, also known as the Queen Charlotte Islands, an archipelago they inhabit, along with non-natives, off Prince Rupert, also in northern

British Columbia. Some 50 other First Nations land claims are outstanding in the province.

The Aboriginals of the Prairies face a gloomier situation than their British Columbian compatriots. Relegated to bleak lands in the late 19th century, after giving up their vast ancestral hunting grounds, these former nomads, who were forced to settle in one place, never really adapted to their new way of life. Serious drug and alcohol problems are undermining these individuals and communities.

The gradual disappearance of traditional grounds has given rise to aggressive territorial claims in most of Canada's provinces. With the help of the Assembly of First Nations, made up of several band chiefs, the First Nations are trying to advance their cause with government authorities, both federal and provincial.

▼ A western Canadian Aboriginal man in ceremonial dress. © *Pierre Longnus*

Aboriginal Art

Totemic culture is surely one of the greatest legacies of Canada's First Nations. This culture reached its height at the middle of the 19th century, and it is easy to imagine the wonder that the sight of 30 to 40 totem poles along the rivers leading to each Aboriginal village must have engendered in the first Europeans to settle in British Columbia. The totems were not revered like idols but featured elements relating to Aboriginal beliefs.

Unfortunately, totem poles do not stand up well against the ravages of weather, and those that have survived to this day have been preserved in parks and museums; there are also some standing in Gwaii Haanas National Park Reserve, under the watchful protection of the Haida Watchmen. Aboriginal art has always been linked to the beliefs of its producers, which were consistently viewed with suspicion by European missionaries, who did all they could to convert Aboriginal people. This ultimately led to a loss of interest in their art among Aboriginals themselves. Efforts were made in the 1960s and 1970s to revive First Nations' cultures in northwestern British Columbia with the Ksan project, which led to the creation of a Native heritage site.

Aboriginal works were long considered anthropological specimens and collected almost exclusively by museums of ethnography. During the 20th century, they gradually came to be recognized as works of art. This art has been the object of growing interest on the part of Canadians since the 1960s. Today, more that 100 Canadian museums have Aboriginal art collections. The artistic practices vary enormously by region. Inuit art and the art of other Aboriginal peoples, in particular, differ in a number of ways.

The 1950s marked a major turning point in Inuit art, as cooperatives to promote and distribute the arts of the Far North were created. Works had previously been small: toys, tools and sacred amulets. The end of the 1940s saw sculptures like those we see today, i.e. up to a metre high in a wide variety of forms and colours. These sculptures can be made of stone, bone or ivory (the use of which is prohibited today), tine or, more uncommonly, tusks or wood. However, engraving and printmaking are more recent practices that are very popular because of the purity of the lines of the works and the quality of their execution. Certains forms of Inuit art are exclusively feminine, including basketwork, dolls, sewing, embroidery, beadwork and work with skins and leather.

Southern Aboriginal peoples practice less sculpture than their northern neighbours, except on the West Coast, a region that is known mainly for its totem poles. In Eastern and Northern Canada tiny works of art reign—and for good reason: most First Nations were nomadic—but the same cannot be said for the Aboriginal peoples of

▲   An animal figure on a totem pole.
    © iStockphoto.com / M. Gillespie

the Pacific Coast. Totem poles represent the lineage of different groups and can be as tall as 20 to 25m. Their designs are drawn from the worlds of spirits, animals and mythology. Generally speaking, Aboroginal works of art are made from materials such as wood, leather or cloth. Aboriginal artists create many three-dimensional works (masks, "dreamcatchers," ornate objects), silkscreen prints and drawings.

▲   Aboriginal jewellery. © Pierre Longnus

Aboriginal Art

THE TOTEM POLES OF
THE NORTHWESTERN FIRST NATIONS

Sculpted using towering cedars and used in the ceremonial potlatches of Aboriginal family clans from the Northwest, totem poles are historical family emblems. They were placed in front of the entrance to the family "longhouse" to honour ancestors, display the clan's status and describe a memorable ceremony or spiritual experience. The totem pole is thus a symbol of the qualities, experience and exploits of the clan.

The images that are sculpted into a totem pole recall a history which can only be read by those who understand the meanings that are attributed to the animals, fish, birds and designs that they depict, as well as their placement on the pole.

Unlike what is commonly thought, the figures on a totem pole do not represent gods; totem poles are not adored as religious icons or used as talismans, and have never been used to ward off evil spirits. Totem poles are similar to heraldic figures or coats of arms and their symbolism. The meaning of the symbols and blazons that distinguish a family, a city or a country are similar to the figures on the totem pole, except that they identify a clan instead.

Northwestern First Nations Symbols and their Meaning

Bear:	strength, acquired humility, maternity, teaching
Beaver:	creativity, artistic ability and determination
Bumblebee:	honesty, purity of thought—good will and instinct
Copper:	wealth and prestige
Crow:	creativity and knowledge—bringer of light
Dove:	love, gentleness and kindness
Dragonfly:	life in constant change
Eagle:	great strength, authority and prestige
Eagle feather:	good luck to the giver and the recipient
Falcon:	strength and foresight
Frog:	spring and renewed life—communicator, firmness
Halibut:	protector of life, strength and firmness
Heron:	patience, grace and accommodation
Hummingbird:	love, beauty, intelligence, spiritual messenger
Killer whale:	traveller and keeper—a symbol of good
Kingfisher:	luck, patience, speed and agility
Loon:	peace, tranquillity—generous by nature
Moon:	nighttime protector and keeper of the earth
Otter:	confident, curious and talented—loyal friendship
Owl:	wisdom
Salmon:	reliability and renewal—a provider
Seal:	brilliant, curious, organized
Spiny dogfish:	perseverance and strength—a born leader
Sun:	healing energy, daytime keeper of earth
Wolf:	intelligence and authority—strong sense of family

Visual Arts

At the beginning of the 20th century, **Emily Carr**, who had travelled extensively throughout British Columbia, produced magnificently beautiful paintings reflecting the splendid landscapes of the Pacific coast and revealing certain aspects of Aboriginal spirituality. Her blues and greens portray the captivating atmosphere of British Columbia.

Several rooms at the Vancouver Art Gallery are devoted exclusively to her work. A pioneer of the West Coast art scene, she was followed by such great artists as **Jack Shadbolt** and **Gordon Smith**, whose work illustrates the unique vision that all inhabitants of this region have of the landscapes that surround them.

▼ A magnificent painting by Emily Carr. © *Emily Carr, Above the Gravel Pit, 1937, oil on canvas, Vancouver Art Gallery Collection, Emily Carr Trust, VAG 42.3.30. Photo: Trevor Mills*

Literature

David Thompson authored one of the earliest pieces of literature from the Canadian West, *David Thompson's Narrative of his Explorations in Western North American 1784-1812*. **Earle Birney** was born in Alberta in 1904, and was brought up there and in British Columbia. His belief that geography links people to their history is evident in his poetry and its attempts to define the significance of place and time.

Born in 1920 in the Yukon, which was overrun by gold-diggers in the 19th century, to a father who participated in the Klondike gold rush, **Pierre Berton** lived in Vancouver for many years. He has written many accounts of the high points of Canadian history, including *The Last Spike*, which recounts the construction of the pan-Canadian railway across the Rockies all the way to Vancouver.

Renowned for her powerful paintings of Canada's Pacific coast, **Emily Carr** completed her first book at the age of 70, just a few years before her death. The few books she wrote are autobiographical works, which vividly portray the atmosphere of British Columbia and exhibit her extensive knowledge of the customs and beliefs of the First Nations.

Robert Kroetch and **Rudy Wiebe** are two of Alberta's most well-respected writers. Kroetch is a storyteller above all, and his *Out West* trilogy offers an in-depth look at Alberta over four decades. *Alberta* is part travel guide, part wonderful collection of stories and essays, and captures the essence of the land and people of Alberta. *Seed Catalogue* is another of his excellent works. Rudy Wiebe was born in Saskatchewan in 1934, but has spent most of his life in Alberta. He was raised as a Mennonite, and the moral vision instilled in him by his religious background is the most important feature of his writing. *The*

EMILY CARR

Literature

► Gabrielle Roy (1909-1983).
© *Archives Canada; NL-022064*

Temptations of Big Bear, for which he won the Governor General's Award, describes the disintegration of native culture as a result of the growth of the Canadian nation.

In 1945, the Franco-Manitoban **Gabrielle Roy** published one of the great classics of French Canadian literature: *Bonheur d'occasion (The Tin Flute)*. Many other works followed, making her one of the Canada's most celebrated authors.

Nancy Huston was born in Calgary, where she lived for 15 years. More than 20 years ago, after a five-year stay in New York City, she decided to relocate to Paris, where she finished her doctoral studies in semiology under the tutelage of Roland Barthes. After winning the Governor General's Award in 1993 for her novel *Cantique des Plaines* (*Plainsong*) she became a major contributor to French-language literature. Though an anglophone, she writes first in French and then translates her own work into English. She has since written several other successful works.

The writings of **Jane Rule**, an American who has lived in British Columbia since 1956, reflect a mentality that is typical of both the American and Canadian west. However, she is better known for her efforts to bridge the gap between the homosexual and heterosexual communities.

▲ Nancy Huston. © *Monique Dykstra / Metropolis Bleu*

Vancouver can be proud of its native son, **Douglas Coupland**, who published his first novel, *Generation X*, in 1991 at the age of 30. His work coined a new catch-phrase that is now used by everyone from sociologists to ad agencies to describe this young, educated and underemployed generation. Coupland has since shifted focus somewhat, having taken to photography and writing about his city and his country. In *City of Glass*, published in 2000, Coupland writes with typical humour and irony about his home town and accompanies his texts with his own photographs. He has also published numerous other works.

Other notable western writers include poets **Patrick Lane** from British Columbia and **Sid Marty** from Alberta.

Vancouver playwright **George Ryga**'s play *Ecstasy of Rita Joe* marked a renewal for Canadian theatre in 1967. This work deals with the culture shock experienced by Aboriginal communities, who are inherently turned towards nature yet existing in a dehumanized western society. Albertan **Brad Fraser**'s powerful play *Unidentified Human Remains and the True Nature of Love* analyzes contemporary love in an urban setting. The play was adapted for the cinema by Québec filmmaker Denys Arcand under the title *Love and Human Remains*.

Music

Western Canada is a cultured place with orchestras, operas and theatre. In the case of Alberta, however, country music is perhaps more representative of the culture. This music has recently experienced a revival, entering the mainstream and moving up all sorts of country charts as well as pop charts. Calgarian **Wilf Carter** (1904-1996) became famous in the United States as a yodelling cowboy. **k.d. lang**, of Consort, Alberta, became a Grammy-winning superstar in the 1990s. In her early days with the Reclines she was known for her outrageous outfits and honky-tonk style, but of late, her exceptional voice and blend of country and pop are her trademarks. A rarity in show business, she has always had the courage to be open about her homosexuality. Alberta also has its share of more mainstream stars, among them **Jann Arden** and relative newcomer **Leslie Feist**, who was born in Nova Scotia but raised in Calgary.

▶ Joni Mitchell. © *Archives Canada; PA-211916*

Loreena McKennitt, whose recordings featuring haunting Celtic melodies have sold by the million in over 40 countries, was born and raised in Morden, Manitoba. **Chantal Kreviazuk**, a Juno-award-winning (the Canadian equivalent of the Grammy) songstress and pianist, hails from Winnipeg, as do the **Crash Test Dummies**, whose first hit was the catchy *Superman's Song* in 1991.

As for Saskatchewan, its most famous daughter by far is popular folk singer **Joni Mitchell**. Born Joan Anderson in Fort McLeod, Alberta, Mitchell grew up in Saskatoon, Saskatchewan before heading south of the border, where she found fame and fortune.

British Columbia, and more particularly cosmopolitan Vancouver, has produced a variety of significant musical acts.

In addition to well-established stars such as **Bryan Adams** (actually born in Kingston, Ontario, but a longtime resident of Vancouver) and jazz singer and pianist **Diana Krall** (born in Nanaimo and the winner of three Juno Awards in 2002 for *The Look of Love*), several young musicians and groups have received critical and commercial success outside the country's borders in recent years. To name but a few, these include pop singer **Nelly Furtado** and musical acts **New Pornographers**, **Be Good Tanyas**, **Hot Hot Heat**, **Black Mountain** and **Destroyer**. Other well-established acts such as **Sarah McLachlan**, **No Means No**, **SNFU**, **DOA** and **Skinny Puppy** have been releasing albums for several years now and have influenced British Columbia's younger generation of musicians.

Movies

Cinema has always been a part of daily life in Vancouver. A day doesn't go by when there isn't a film crew on one of Vancouver's streets. Studios have been established in North Vancouver and it's no longer surprising to run into Hollywood stars in the city's streets or shops. Every autumn, the Vancouver International Film Festival offers some 150 quality foreign films, much to the pleasure of film buffs.

▼ Film-making in Vancouver. © Jack Rowand

The Wines of British Columbia

▲   The fruits of a bountiful harvest.
© Pierre Longnus

operations, modernized their equipment and hired the best grape growers from wine regions in the Americas and Europe.

When you visit British Columbia's "wine country," you'll get to meet grape growers and their teams and discover a surprising range of award-winning wines that are ringing in a new era for the province's wine industry. The VQA seal is issued to wines that have achieved a certain level of quality. Wines that carry the VQA seal are made according to strict standards and are tasted by a jury of experts before being approved by the British Columbia Wine Institute.

British Columbia's wines are increasing in popularity, not only in Western Canada, but also around the world. After the adoption of provincial regulations on the quality of wine in 1990, sales increased, and the region's grands crus carved out an enviable reputation, receiving positive reviews. The VQA program, for Vintners Quality Alliance, was a driving force behind the revival of this still-expanding industry.

The wine industry in British Columbia has been revitalized thanks to the skills and devotion of a new generation of wine growers. They have planted the most suitable types of vines for the land, and wineries have expanded their

WINE COUNTRY

British Columia's wineries are located in two distinct production regions: the southern part of Vancouver Island, and the Fraser, Okanagan and Similkameen valleys in the southern part of the province.

Vancouver Island, located off the coast of continental British Columbia, is the newest wine region in the province. Around one hour from the capital of Victoria, the island's hillside wineries wind along small country roads that connect historic towns. Over 20ha of

The Wines of British Columbia

▲ Wine-making season in British Columbia. © *British Columbia Wine Institute*

grapes are planted in the southeastern part of the island, near the city of Duncan.

The Fraser Valley, a farming community with fertile land, stretches east in the city of Vancouver; the province's largest agricultural area, it is growing rapidly. There are currently some 20ha of grapes and two wineries less than a half-hour's drive from Vancouver. This coastal production region enjoys warm, rainy winters and hot, dry summers. As in the backcountry (Okanagan-Similkameen), irrigation is required for grape growing.

The interior of British Columbia is home to the largest and oldest wine region of the province: the Okanagan Valley. This magnificent valley, some 150km long, is dotted with over 30 wineries with around 1,200ha of land planted with top-quality vines. The south of the valley, which receives less than 15cm of rain per year, is Canada's only classified

desert area. For its part, the north of the valley receives less than 40cm of rain. The sout is mainly planted with classic red vinifera grapes, while French and German varietals of white grapes are planted in the north.

West of the Okanagan Valley, across the mountains, is the desert highland growing region of the Similkameen Valley. Nestled along the picturesque Similkameen River and surrounded by steep mountains, the region's two wineries have 16ha of grapes planted along the banks of the river.

The climate of the Okanagan and Similkameen valleys is the result of their location on the leeward side of the Coast Mountains. These valleys benefit from warm, dry summers, long periods of sun and low humidity.

▸ A hillside vineyard overlooking Lake Okanagan. © *Cedar Creek Estate Winery / Brian Sprout*

pages 284-285

▸ Banff National Park, the best-known and most popular of all of Canada's national parks. © *iStockphoto.com / Elizabeth Quilliam*

pages 286

▸ Yoho National Park. © *Philippe Renault*

The Wines of British Columbia

Index

Contact Information

Offices

Canada: Ulysses Travel Guides, 4176 St. Denis Street, Montréal, Québec, H2W 2M5, ☎514-843-9447, ▤514-843-9448, info@ulysses.ca, www.ulyssesguides.com

Europe: Les Guides de Voyage Ulysse SARL, 127 Rue Amelot, 75011 Paris, France, ☎01 43 38 89 50, voyage@ulysse.ca, www.ulyssesguides.com

Distributors

U.S.A.: Hunter Publishing, 130 Campus Drive, Edison, NJ 08818, ☎800-255-0343, ▤(732) 417-1744 or 0482, comments@hunterpublishing.com, www.hunterpublishing.com

Canada: Ulysses Travel Guides, 4176 St. Denis Street, Montréal, Québec, H2W 2M5, ☎514-843-9882, ext. 2232, ▤514-843-9448, info@ulysses.ca, www.ulyssesguides.com

Great Britain and Ireland: Roundhouse Publishing, Millstone, Limers Lane, Northam, North Devon, EX39 2RG, ☎1 202 66 54 32, ▤1 202 66 62 19, roundhouse.group@ukgateway.net

Other countries: Ulysses Travel Guides, 4176 St. Denis Street, Montréal, Québec, H2W 2M5, ☎514-843-9882, ext.2232, ▤514-843-9448, info@ulysses.ca, www.ulyssesguides.com